THE
PLATFORM
PARADOX

Mauro F. Guillén

THE PLATFORM PARADOX

How Digital Businesses Succeed in
an Ever-Changing Global Marketplace

WHARTON
SCHOOL
PRESS

Philadelphia

Published by Wharton School Press
The Wharton School
University of Pennsylvania
3620 Locust Walk
300 Steinberg Hall-Dietrich Hall
Philadelphia, PA 19104
Email: whartonschoolpress@wharton.upenn.edu
Website: wsp.wharton.upenn.edu

Ebook ISBN: 978-1-61363-115-7
Paperback ISBN: 978-1-61363-116-4

Contents

Introduction
The Dawn of a New Age

The year was 1995. The internet age was dawning. A new digital company presented itself to the world as "Earth's Biggest Bookstore." It enabled purchasing books through a series of clicks, culminating in the physical delivery of the product. The customer could even have it wrapped as a gift before it was shipped to its recipient.

By the end of 2020, that digital company was worth $1.6 trillion, generating revenues of nearly $350 billion and employing more than 1 million people worldwide. It was engaged in the digital sale and physical distribution of not just books but all manner of goods, in addition to offering a marketplace, web services, and audiovisual content creation and distribution. Far from being a purely virtual company, it had amassed half a billion square feet of storage and logistics space—roughly equivalent to all the office space in Manhattan. The company launched many other innovations, including one-click purchasing (1997), a premium membership program with free delivery (2005), the e-reader (2007), and same-day delivery (2015), among many other firsts.[1]

People often mention that Amazon faces stiff competition in cloud computing (Microsoft Azure and Google Cloud) and video streaming (Netflix), but it continues to dwarf competitors in ecommerce such as Walmart, Etsy, and Shopify. Its core platform offers over 350 million products from nearly 2 million companies, both large and small, which gives it a unique view into what consumers like and don't like. The company makes it nearly impossible for even the most powerful brands in the world to skew its platform. "Amazon is the gatekeeper," Scott Heedham, whose company BuyBoxer sells toys, sporting goods, and more, told the *New Yorker*. "It makes all the rules."

Making all the rules inevitably raises the specter of antitrust investigations because of uncompetitive behavior. Amazon has been accused of unfair labor practices, turning a blind eye to counterfeit merchandise, and copying products for its AmazonBasics line. Many people deplore the fact that downtown areas are increasingly populated by empty storefronts while online retailers proliferate endlessly. Yet, Amazon seems poised to continue expanding in scale and scope, especially in the age of social distancing and remote work from the home.

Here's the paradox, however. For all its size, clout, and growth potential, Amazon derives 61% of its revenue from the US market, which represents less than 20% of the global economy. Its reach among internet users in the United States is about 75%. The company is not universally successful. In no country other than its own does it have more than a 50% market share in any category. In China, soon to become the world's largest consumer market, its market share is a mere 0.4%. The Chinese companies Taobao and Tmall dwarf Amazon in total size as marketplaces. On the whole, Amazon accounts for just over half of the digital market in the United States, but only about 6% globally. Amazon could reach half of humanity in about 60 national markets. By contrast, one can enjoy a Coke in more than 200 countries and territories—meaning everywhere.

I wrote this book for two reasons. The first is that digital platforms are changing the rules of competition in the global economy. The world's seven largest companies in terms of market capitalization are platform businesses in full or in part: Apple, Microsoft, Amazon, Alphabet, Alibaba, Facebook, and Tencent. It's a brave new world dominated by companies based in the United States and China, which dwarf their competitors in terms of R&D investment, cloud traffic, unique visitors, revenue, and profits. Until recently, it took *Fortune* 500 companies an average of 20 years to reach billion-dollar market valuations. Successful platforms reach that milestone in an average of four years.[2] Digital platforms have led to a transformation of nearly every aspect of economic and social life, from retail trade and employment services to personal relationships and payment methods. In addition, established companies with traditional business models have jumped on the bandwagon by creating platforms of their own.

The second motivation came from a mundane observation: Most platforms considered to be successful have triumphed in only some, rather than all, parts of the world—like Amazon. There are very few truly global digital platforms. In my more than three decades of studying multinational firms in industries such as apparel, automobiles, and banking, I found that they often misunderstood key aspects of what it takes to succeed globally, from culture and institutions to local competitive dynamics and pursuing markets in a logical sequence. Seeing multibillion-dollar companies like Amazon flounder in certain markets presented me with the opportunity to explore the limitations of different types of global strategies. People often assume platform businesses always become globally dominated by a company that ruthlessly exploits early-mover advantages, winner-take-all dynamics, tipping points, economies of scale, and network effects.

The platform paradox refers to a very basic observation and yields a disarmingly simple yet effective way of overcoming it. The observation, as illustrated by the example of Amazon, is that most platforms fail to reach anything that approaches global ubiquity. Many of them can be perfectly successful and profitable without dominating the entire market—something that will also help them avoid accusations of anticompetitive behavior. The only way for platforms to reach their growth potential before a competitor steals the opportunity is to (1) diagnose the underlying network effects, (2) assess the potential single-side, same-side, and cross-side dynamics, and (3) prioritize growth efforts by geography in a way that network effects are maximized over time. The success of digital platforms is, ultimately, a process and not a destination.

I decided to research dozens of digital platforms, talk to their managers, and collect information on their presence around the world. I was looking for an explanation as to why and how some of them have succeeded in different national markets to a much greater extent than others, in the hope of formulating a framework for managing platforms across national borders. This book is the result of that search.

Network Effects and International Strategy

Digital platforms bring together users like individuals and businesses, and the more individuals and businesses there are, the stronger the so-called network effects. The fundamental insight in this book is that all network effects are not created equal. For user A of a given digital platform, the value of an additional user B located in a different part of the world may be large or small, depending on the nature of the network effect.

Consider the situation in which user A would like to hail a ride from home to the local railway station at a particular moment in time. User A's chances of getting a ride within a minute or two are not affected by user B's need for a ride, unless that user is in the vicinity. Moreover, ride hailing is a two-sided network, with drivers and riders looking for a match at the local level. Thus, the number of drivers in the streets looking for a passenger in user B's location is not relevant to user A's either.

This is an example of a *local* network effect. By contrast, there are many situations in which the network effects operate at the *global* level or at a level somewhere in between—like the *national* or *regional* level. The level at which network effects operate shapes which strategy may be the best one to make a digital platform successful across a variety of national markets. This is the fundamental insight in this book.

I begin my analysis in chapter 1 by taking stock of the growth of the global digital economy, the demographics of digital use, and the ways in which the COVID-19 pandemic has accelerated digitization. There are considerable differences not just in terms of the development of the digital economy around the world but also in terms of cultural and regulatory aspects.

In chapter 2 I dig deeper into the nature of network effects, drawing a distinction between one-sided and two-sided network effects, on the one hand, and local, national, regional, and global network effects, on the other. This dual distinction becomes the foundation for determining which is the best growth strategy. Each type of network effect calls for a different strategy, and I illustrate the dynamics with two cases of local network effects, Tinder and Uber, and several instances of global network effects, such as TransferWise in international remittance services.

Chapter 3 is devoted to the digital transformation of traditional businesses. I analyze the cases of apparel (Zara), retail (Walmart), and toys (Lego) and examine why digitalization has failed in the instances of books and wine. In other sectors, I show that successful digitalization and platform growth have occurred only in isolated cases, like the *New York Times* in the printed news media.

In chapter 4 I deal with the internationalization of digital platforms, focusing on Airbnb. I debunk the myth that success in one country, however large, means success in the world as a whole, and examine the circumstances under which it is possible to deploy a global strategy that takes into consideration local peculiarities.

In chapter 5 we will examine the possibilities of and limits to global expansion with the cases of Skype, Zoom, and Spotify. The way people use platforms and the cultural variations underlying such use turn out to be a major factor in international expansion.

Finally, I conclude the book by offering an integrated framework for identifying and implementing a digital platform strategy across geographies. I also offer recommendations as to the best international strategies to thrive under different types of network effects.

Chapter 1

The Rise of Digital Platforms

The recorded music industry has gone through a number of technological disruptions since the invention of the phonograph in 1877. Vinyl records and cassettes dominated the post–World War II period. By the 1980s and 1990s, compact discs had taken over. At the turn of the twenty-first century, music downloads and streaming started to grow, eventually capturing two-thirds of the market.[3]

Music streaming has revolutionized consumption because it is all about access, not ownership. It offers instant gratification and mobility. Most importantly, it is a platform supporting an entire ecosystem that generates value for an expansive number of participants, including listeners, artists, music labels, influencers, and concert organizers. In addition, telecommunications carriers and mobile-phone manufacturers also participate by preinstalling the app of a streaming service to make their offerings more attractive.

But the most consequential feature of music streaming is the wealth of individual and situational information gathered in the process, which can be used to fine-tune offerings, build playlists, and attract advertisers. Most music streaming platforms—Spotify (the global market leader); QQ Music, KuGou, and Kuwo (all owned by China's Tencent); India's Gaana; or South Korea's MelOn—offer seamless connectivity through social media platforms like Facebook or WeChat, enabling users to share songs and their feelings about them, exchange information on upcoming concerts, and pursue their musical tastes. Producing, distributing, and enjoying music have become fully integrated into the platform economy.

Platforms have transformed the ways in which consumers and businesses interact. Today, a digitally connected consumer can listen to a news aggregator while taking a shower, consult the weather, hail a ride, secure a restaurant reservation, hold a remote work meeting, contribute to a philanthropic cause, find a date, exchange photos with family and friends, share the cost of a meal, and listen to music. In doing so, platform users leave a long trail of digital footprints about their daily behavior and whereabouts. The data are relational, in the sense that the user is establishing and acting on relationships with other users and with many different kinds of organizations.

The digital platforms that facilitate such contacts and transactions use a panoply of technologies including big data analytics, machine learning, cloud computing, and the blockchain, among others. All-digital interactions provide a seemingly endless stream of data to feed the nervous system of the platforms, propelling them to even higher levels of reach and accuracy. Their success, however, depends on correctly identifying the nature of those interconnections and on making strategic decisions consistent with them.

What Are Digital Platforms?

Digital platforms come in many shapes and sizes, but they all share three basic features. First, they offer users some kind of technology-enabled interaction for the purpose of obtaining or accomplishing something useful and valuable. This expanding universe includes social platforms like Facebook or WeChat, where people establish and grow relationships with other users; marketplaces like Amazon or Shopify, where sellers and buyers meet; streaming platforms like Netflix or Spotify, where users can enjoy audiovisual content; crowdsourcing platforms like Uber or Airbnb, which offer mutually convenient ways of exchanging value; telecommunications and telework platforms like Zoom or DocuSign; and so on. Some platforms enable individuals, companies, or organizations to build their own platforms within the platforms, as in the cases of social platforms and marketplaces.

The second key characteristic of digital platforms is that the value the platform offers to each user grows with the number of people and/or companies that use it. This is the famous *network effect*, which carries three implications:

- In principle, platforms can scale up indefinitely without any signs of performance decline.
- First movers can reap enormous economies of scale and thus create barriers to entry.
- A large user base of loyal and/or captive users creates phenomenal opportunities for revenue diversification.

The third prominent feature of digital platforms is that they can accommodate different kinds of revenue models. On Spotify, for instance, users can enjoy streamed music for free if they are willing to listen to an occasional advertisement. Or they can pay a monthly subscription fee to listen ad-free. One can also use a social platform for free and be able to interact with other users, but pay for premium services. If the platform has two or more different types of users, it is possible to subsidize one of them.

Given the three basic characteristics of digital platforms, most people are surprised to learn that there are very few truly global platforms—platforms with a presence and a user base *across the entire world*. If it weren't for government regulation, Google would be an example of a global platform, with a worldwide market share in searches hovering around 90%. Facebook, with a 60% world market share, is also a platform that is nearly global in geographical scope.

Now consider other platforms that, in spite of their multibillion-dollar valuations, are very far from being global. Uber is a behemoth in the United States, disrupting one industry after another—how we get around, how we get our food, and even how cities provide more mobility to their residents. For all its might and potential, Uber has failed to reach critical mass in most African markets, in India, and in China, where it sold its incipient operations to Didi, a huge local competitor.

This is a familiar story for many different kinds of platforms. Spotify, a Swedish company, is the global market leader in music streaming. It has a strong footprint in Europe, the United States, and Latin America but only a token presence in the emerging markets of Asia, the Middle East, and Africa.

The fact that, in spite of their awesome power, most digital platforms find it hard to succeed in every market around the world raises several important questions. Is it due to the uneven and asynchronous worldwide development of the internet? Is it the result of government regulation or barriers to free trade and free investment? Or is it because of the intrinsic characteristics of the platform businesses themselves? The answer to this puzzle is that all three factors play a role in preventing platforms from succeeding across the board, in every national market, and across market segments.

Digital platforms collect, store, and analyze information with the purpose of monetizing it. Data monetization can take place in a variety of ways, but always by bringing users together so that they can interact with one another. Platforms add value in different ways:

- Facilitating relationships among people and organizations (Google, Facebook, Twitter, LinkedIn, WeChat)
- Enabling buyers and sellers to conclude transactions in exchange for a fee (Amazon, Alibaba, Shopify)
- Inviting people to share each other's assets (Uber, Didi, Airbnb)
- Connecting people for other social, learning, or work purposes (Tinder, Zoom, TaskRabbit)
- Producing and selling content in the form of information, text, audio, and/or video (BuzzFeed, Coursera, Netflix, Spotify)
- Intermediating and disintermediating money and finance (Alipay, PayPal, Venmo)
- Renting cloud services (Amazon, Microsoft)[4]

Digital platforms are not the exclusive province of start-ups. Most large, established companies, and quite a few smaller ones, have created platforms. Many manufacturing firms have created marketplaces for their suppliers and crowdsourcing platforms for solving complex engineering problems, for instance. Within the service sector, all manner of companies have established platforms to interact with customers, suppliers, and society in general, especially in areas like banking, insurance, travel, media, and entertainment. Oftentimes, established firms launch platforms in response to the disruption and competitive threats from start-ups.

The nonprofit sector has also moved swiftly to embrace digital platforms, with the aim of improving the state of the world. Examples include exchange, donation, crowdsourcing, education, service, and sharing platforms. Perhaps the most famous example is Wikipedia, which has transformed the way people access and share knowledge on a truly encyclopedic scale.

Governments have also created digital platforms, though mostly for the purpose of facilitating the relationship between citizens, residents, or taxpayers and various agencies and departments, and only rarely to encourage user-to-user interaction, as in public spheres for political deliberation, policy consultation, and voter engagement. Governments have also created platforms to encourage citizens to engage in appropriate behaviors during emergencies. Needless to say, political candidates use platforms to their advantage. Finally, multilateral organizations such as the World Bank have launched crowdfunding and knowledge-dissemination platforms.

If the Digital Economy Is Not Flat, the Platform Economy Isn't Either

The COVID-19 pandemic has made readily apparent the longstanding fact that the digital economy is not of one piece. For instance, not everyone can work remotely from home through some kind of digital platform. In the United States, the work-from-home option applies to fewer than 40% of workers.[5]

There is considerable cross-national heterogeneity in terms of the usage of the fixed and mobile internet by socioeconomic group, age, gender, race, and ethnicity. In addition, governments regulate data privacy and intellectual property in different ways, resulting in a situation in which platforms need to adapt to local peculiarities. Moreover, network effects range in terms of geographical scope, from local to global.

The use of different modes of access to the world of information offered by the internet varies widely. While nearly everyone in developed markets has access to a mobile network, in the less developed parts of the world—sub-Saharan Africa, parts of the Middle East, and parts of South Asia—about three in four people have a mobile phone, but only one in three has a mobile broadband connection. The quality of the connection is also unevenly distributed, with 20% of people in emerging markets and 60% in the least developed countries lacking access to an LTE (Long-Term Evolution) or WiMAX (Worldwide Interoperability for Microwave Access) network or better, compared with only 7% in developed countries.[6]

While mobile phones can be used to access most digital platforms, some are easier to use with a computer, especially those that facilitate working or learning remotely. The problem is that access to a fixed broadband connection is much less prevalent, with only a third of people in developed markets having one, 10% in emerging markets, and barely 2% in the less developed parts of the world. Moreover, the proportion of households with a computer hovers around 85% in most developed countries but is as low as 18% in Africa. Another important concern is the cost of broadband access, which can be 10 or even 20 times higher in developing countries than in developed markets, adjusted for the level of income.

These differences have two implications for digital businesses. The world is not flat, at least in the sense that markets cannot be approached in exactly the same way. Not only are some markets limited in their potential, but businesses also need to tailor offerings given the prevalence of different devices, download speeds, and locations where people access online services. The second implication is that local competitors may know how to navigate those constraints better than global companies, which need to resort to alliances or acquisitions to overcome the disadvantage.

There are also persistent differences in access to the digital world by income, gender, and age. In the developed countries, the bottom quarter of households by income tend not to have fixed broadband or computers. Men are 2 or 3 percentage points ahead of women, a difference that can be as high as 15 percentage points in some parts of the Middle East and Africa. This gap limits the labor market opportunities of women, as well as constrains their ability to become entrepreneurs. Given that men and women behave differently as consumers, the gender digital divide is yet another factor for firms to consider in their strategizing. Like gender, age is another important factor behind patterns of digital consumption. The born-digital generations are far more likely to use platforms than are senior citizens, with baby boomers falling somewhere in between.

In addition to differences by country, income, age, and gender, the global development of digital platforms occurs in a landscape in which national borders matter because of regulation. Governments differ massively in terms of their regulatory approaches to web neutrality, data privacy, freedom of expression, freedom of the media, and intellectual property protections. In most cases, large differences by country do not imply a slower growth of platform businesses. However, such variations spell trouble for global platforms while helping local platforms prosper.

Thus, successful strategies in one market may not easily transfer to another in which government regulations are different. Moreover, a business model that works wonders in a market characterized by lax regulations about data privacy and constraints on freedom of expression may not "travel" well in another market with the opposite features. As in any other part of the economy, regulatory fragmentation favors local competitors and multilocal firms that, while operating in different markets, tailor their approaches to each market based on local characteristics.

The Impact of COVID-19

The COVID-19 pandemic has added urgency to the study of digital platforms given how ubiquitous they have become in the age of lockdowns and social distancing. Remote work—which before the crisis was the norm for only about 3% of American workers—became a new reality for tens of millions of individuals. With some companies switching almost completely to remote work, and about one in three Americans performing their duties from home, platforms such as Zoom or DocuSign saw demand for their services explode. In addition, remote learning by tens of millions of students provided an additional impetus to the growth of digital platforms.

The lockdown also introduced new opportunities in ecommerce, completely unanticipated by giants like Amazon or Alibaba. For instance, the Canadian digital marketplace Shopify has attracted many small businesses that sell to consumers within a distance of 15 miles. This kind of short-distance ecommerce has blossomed. Moving nimbly to nurture this new source of business, Shopify offers small businesses a complete suite of services not limited to a mere storefront. It also helps vendors monitor costs, pay bills, plan for deliveries, and optimize overall cash flows.

The shortening of supply chains to make them more resilient to unforeseen events like a natural disaster or pandemic has multiplied the possibilities of using blockchain platforms to manage complex interactions between companies and their suppliers. Given the renewed emphasis on product provenance, the blockchain offers a secure platform to ensure the efficiency of the supply chain and that customers are satisfied with their purchases.

Other types of platforms have also seen enormous growth in the wake of COVID-19, including streaming services like Spotify and Netflix, and delivery platforms like Grubhub or Uber Eats. By contrast, dating apps and all platforms dedicated to events and tourism have struggled to remain relevant in the new reality of travel limitations and social distancing. But as chapter 4 shows, many of them have found a way to adapt. For instance, Airbnb has turned to other areas of growth while the economy is recovering and travel is beginning to resume. Perhaps the most decisive aspect accounting for the growth of digital platforms during the lockdown is their inherent power to help people stay connected with one another and with the companies and organizations they interact with on a daily basis.

The COVID-19 pandemic, however, has tended to increase the digital divide, especially by income, gender, race, and ethnicity. Access to remote work is unevenly distributed, and the lockdowns have changed the volume of household tasks and their allocation by gender. The pandemic has also brought to the fore racial and ethnic differences in access to online services in countries such as Brazil, Mexico, and the United States.

The Platform Paradox: Things to Remember

- Digital platforms create ecosystems in which a variety of actors create value for one another based on the vast amounts of information collected.
- Platforms grow on the basis of network effects that attract new participants, reduce unit costs, and provide for strong first-mover advantages.
- The platform economy is not flat in the sense that national borders and differences by income, age, gender, race, and ethnicity tend to fragment the market.

Chapter 2

The Strategic Management of Network Effects

After enlisting three Estonians to write the code, a Danish-Swedish entrepreneurial duo launched Skype in 2003. The idea was to offer users free audio and video calls over the internet, with the possibility of bringing several people into the conversation, and to exchange text messages, videos, and files. It quickly became a nightmare for those sleepy telephone companies that once upon a time operated as territorial monopolies. Skype's key insight was that the population of users could grow indefinitely without any centralized database or directory. Rather, the user directory would be distributed across the nodes in the network.

Skype's peer-to-peer model, unlike the usual client-server approach followed by the incumbent companies, promised to deliver rapid growth at a low cost. In addition, people could use a conventional phone to dial Skype users. Since speed was of the essence, the platform required no proof of identify in order for someone to join. Strong global network effects would do the rest. In 2011, given the popularity of this platform, the *Oxford English Dictionary* created an entry for the verb "skype," which means to have a spoken conversation over the internet.

Network effects lie at the core of digital platforms. Users flock to platforms in search of value. When it's about to pour rain, some people prefer to hail a ride rather than wait for the bus. Their over-riding concern is to reach their destination on a timely basis while avoiding getting wet. The platform will create value to the extent that enough drivers are in that location to meet demand, which may be achieved through higher prices, which attract more drivers.

Digital platforms have revolutionized personal relationships. Someone who wants to go on a date may use a dating platform, and the idea is to use one that has many other local users so that the probability of a match increases. However, if the goal is to find a suitable person to marry, a local search may be too constraining. Most people would prefer to conduct a national search, and some might pursue a global quest for the right spouse.

People use platforms for various purposes, and they seek to benefit from network effects that operate at different levels. Understanding those network effects is essential to building a strategy that delivers growth across the world.

What Are Network Effects?

Network effects are the main source of value and competitive advantage in digital platforms. A positive network effect occurs when the value of using the platform rises for all as the number of users increases. Robert Metcalfe, the entrepreneur who coinvented the ethernet, noted in the 1980s that there was a nonlinear relationship between the value of a telephone network and the number of telephones connected to it. Metcalfe's law was originally a statement about the number of "compatible communicating devices," not the number of users.[7]

It is important to note the key difference between network effects and *economies of scale*. These are the three most important distinctions to keep in mind:

- Network effects have to do with customer demand, while economies of scale are a characteristic of the way in which a good or service is produced—that is, the supply.
- All digital platforms, however, take advantage of both economies of scale (on the supply side) and network effects

(on the demand side), which may result in strong first-mover advantages, tipping points, and monopolization.

- The two mechanisms are actually interrelated. Thus, users flock to a platform as it grows bigger in order to enjoy the positive network effect, and a larger number of users enables the platform to spread its fixed costs over a larger number of users, thus reaping economies of scale. For instance, the cost of developing the architecture of a digital platform does not increase with the number of users, and thus contributes to creating economies of scale.

Similarly, network effects often become intertwined with *switching costs*. There are several points worth noting:

- Users lose value when they switch to another social platform in which their friends or relatives do not participate.
- Switching costs are lower in payment platforms than in social platforms, unless most of the user's payments or receipts relate to friends or relatives as opposed to vendors.
- In some cases, the switching costs are completely negligible. For example, most drivers and riders have more than one ride-hailing app on their phones, and transfer back and forth in real time to minimize waiting time.

Network effects tend to create strong *first-mover advantages*, whereby the platform that grows the fastest enjoys increased demand, lower costs, and stronger financial performance. First-mover advantages, however, are tricky to manage in the context of a digital platform. Network effects do not necessarily lead to *winner-take-all* dynamics and monopoly rents, for two reasons:

- First, if switching costs are negligible, or if users prefer to participate in several platforms to maximize the benefits of interconnectivity with a larger set of users, user loyalty to a specific platform will be low, and platforms will overlap. For

instance, many people have both Uber and Lyft apps installed on their phones.
- Second, users will participate in multiple platforms if some goods or services are made exclusive on one platform but not on others. An example is the rise in streaming services: Many users have Amazon Prime, Hulu, and Netflix accounts.

It's very important to carefully analyze the interactions among network effects, economies of scale, first-mover advantages, and switching costs when it comes to managing digital platforms on a global scale.

Types of Network Effects

For the purpose of strategy formulation, network effects can be classified in a number of ways:

- First, there are *dyadic* networks, in which interactions take place between pairs of users, and *multiparty* networks, in which interactions can take place among more than two users at a time. An example of a dyadic network is a dating platform, while a videoconferencing platform is a multiparty network.
- Dyadic and multiparty networks can be further subdivided into *unidirectional*, *bidirectional*, or *multidirectional* networks, depending on who can initiate an interaction. Implementing a digital platform with different network characteristics may enable a company to segment the market, differentiate the product, and create value. For example, the dating platform Bumble enables only women to initiate a conversation after a match occurs. In response, Tinder added a similar optional feature for women (My Move).
- A third important classification involves the distinction between *one-sided* and *two-sided* platforms. In a one-sided network, all users belong to the same category. For example,

in a telephone network, all users can either initiate or receive a call. By contrast, in a digital marketplace, there are sellers and buyers. The same applies in a crowdsourcing platform such as those used for ride hailing or accommodation sharing, where we find drivers and riders, and hosts and guests, respectively.

From a strategic point of view, two-sided platforms offer an expanded set of competitive tools, including price discrimination and cross subsidization. There are two golden rules when it comes to pricing. First, platforms should subsidize the most price-sensitive side. And second, platforms should assess a higher price to the side that grows faster in response to growth on the other side. In gaming platforms, for instance, it makes sense to subsidize the gamers by offering them underpriced consoles.

In practice, a two-sided platform can set in motion two different network effects:

- *Same-side* network effects, in which more sellers attract more sellers, or more buyers attract more buyers.
- *Cross-side* network effects, in which more buyers attract more sellers, or more sellers attract more buyers.

Digital platforms can incentivize different network effects while discouraging others by reallocating resources, changing pricing models, and offering special deals or promotions.

Some experts make a further distinction between network effects and virality. Both create value, but in different ways. Virality is often-times used to attract *new* users to a platform, whereas network effects occur to the extent that users have already become part of the platform. But virality can also be used to generate fuss or to insti-gate actions and reactions among users. This is especially the case with social platforms, where news, information, ideas, calls to action, and other types of transmittable items may become viral in the sense of being retransmitted from one user to another.

A positive network effect can turn negative under several circumstances:

- First, if the platform is unable to scale up its resources quickly enough and users are disappointed by the experience.
- Second, if users perceive a lack of exclusivity.
- And third, if users are overwhelmed by the amount of exchange, spam, or traffic on the platform.

The last and most transcendental distinction among different types of network effects involves their geographical scope. Network effects can be *local*, *national*, *regional*, or *global*, depending on the level at which the value of the network to any one user increases with the number of users. As we will see, this distinction has implications for growth strategy, international expansion, and the relationship between the platform and its regulators.

The Geographical Scope of Network Effects

Network effects operate at different geographical levels. *Local network effects* occur when colocation, or proximity, matters.

For instance, ride hailing by definition requires drivers and riders to converge in time and space. Whether the platform has many drivers and would-be riders in another town or country is completely immaterial. If I am in Philadelphia trying to get home on a rainy day after a hard day's work, I could not care less about how many people are using the same app in Sydney, Australia. So while Uber and Cabify have users (drivers and riders) in many countries around the world, both of them base their business on local network effects.

In the case of ride hailing, there is a key asymmetry between network effects and economies of scale. While the network effects are local, the platform might be able to take advantage of a large global user base in terms of spreading fixed costs. For example, the effort involved in developing the algorithms to match drivers with riders *at a particular location in real time* does not have to be replicated for every location in which the platform operates. That fixed cost can be spread among all users around the world.

Another example of a local network effect is Olio, the food-sharing platform. It was launched in 2015 by Tessa Clarke and Saasha Celestial-One to address the problem of food waste. Globally, about 30% of the food that reaches the end consumer is discarded. "We connect neighbors with each other and Food Waste Hero volunteers with local businesses, to share food (and other things) rather than chuck them away," its website reads.

In principle, any Olio user can either donate or receive unwanted foodstuffs, and that's why it is essentially a one-sided platform, in which there are no buyers and sellers. Given that proximity matters for sharing food in the sense that shipping it somewhere else would be costly and counterproductive, the network effects are fundamentally local (unlike in the case of Rent the Runway). If we could avoid wasting nearly one-third of all food, we might be able to reduce carbon emissions considerably, given that food production and distribution contribute about 30% of total worldwide greenhouse gas emissions.

National network effects are at work when users see value in having on the same platform other users from within the boundaries of a certain culture or country, but not beyond. We can appreciate the difference between local and national network effects by considering different kinds of dating platforms:

- Casual dating platforms rely on local network effects, given that most people who use them are not looking for someone with whom to initiate a romantic relationship but rather to meet someone in their vicinity and within a relatively short time frame.
- By contrast, matchmaking platforms attract users who are looking for a romantic relationship with the purpose of establishing a lasting connection to someone else, perhaps even with the final aim of getting married. Given that the vast majority of people prefer to marry someone from their

same culture and/or country, matchmaking platforms are
driven mostly by national network effects: The more people
with certain characteristics from a given country flock
to one platform, the more other people looking for those
characteristics will also join the platform.

It is also possible that *regional network effects* are stronger than
national or global ones, especially within Africa, Asia, Europe, or
Latin America. For instance, in the case of remittance platforms used
by immigrants to send money to family or friends in their country
of origin, local and national network effects are negligible. But
regional network effects are important because about half of immigrants live in a country within the same region as their country of
origin.

The other half of total immigration involves movements of people
across regions of the world. More broadly, *global network effects* occur
when users benefit from other users' presence on the platform,
regardless of location. Teleconferencing and file-sharing platforms
are among the purest examples of a business driven by global network effects. But there is another powerful reason why a platform
can be global in its network effects. We encounter a global network
effect in a two-sided platform whose objective is for the two types
of users to coincide in time and space after a match takes place.
Accommodation-sharing platforms are one such example because
the host (or the property) and the guest need to come together phys-
ically. Users prefer Skype to communicate with others to the extent
its users increase.

The matchmaking example above is based on a very specific
assumption: that users specify their preferences. One of the most
intriguing ways in which digital platforms are changing the world is
by making preference endogenous—by expanding the universe of
possibilities that people wish to contemplate when they purchase
goods and services or when they look for a personal relationship,
romantic or not. While it is too early to tell, it may well be that a
global matchmaking platform could have such a strong influence

over its users that a majority of them start considering romantic relationships with people from a country other than their own.

In other cases, the reason network effects turn out to be national rather than global is because of transportation costs or regulations against the free movement of goods, services, or money. That's why used-item marketplaces like eBay tend to operate on the basis of mostly national network effects, because it is often hard for a seller to send a good to a buyer in a different country.

Facebook is not just a platform with users from all over the world, but also one driven by global network effects. From the point of view of its revenue model, Facebook is a two-sided network, with people who interact with others (friends) on one side, and companies willing to advertise, on the other. Facebook's more than 2.5 billion active users attract advertisers, who spent $70 billion in 2019, nearly 99% of the platform's total revenue.[8] While many small, purely local companies advertise on Facebook, large companies with customers in many countries account for the lion's share.

Platforms come in very different shapes and sizes along a number of dimensions: dyadic or multiparty; unidirectional, bidirectional, or multidirectional; one- or two-sided; and local, national, regional, or global. Figure 2.1 summarizes the two key characteristics we will use to identify the optimal competitive posture, international strategy, and relationships with key stakeholders, including regulators. A one-sided food-sharing platform like Olio capitalizes on local network effects, whereas Skype offers its users connectivity on a global scale. Uber's service requires a critical mass of drivers and

Figure 2.1. Types of Digital Platforms

	Geographical scope of network effects	
	(−) Local →	Global (+)
One-sided	Olio	Skype
Two-sided	Uber	Facebook

riders at the local level, but Facebook enables users to interact among themselves and with advertisers globally.

Note, however, that nothing prevents platforms like Olio or Uber from expanding internationally. In principle, they can set up operations and attract users in as many locations worldwide as they wish. But unlike Skype and Facebook, they need to gain critical mass in each locality. This type of international strategy is called "multi-domestic" or "multilocal," adopted over the years by companies operating in compartmentalized markets.

Local Network Effects: Tinder's Rise to Prominence—and Strategic Challenges

The casual dating platform Tinder was the highest-grossing mobile app in 2019, surpassing powerhouses such as Netflix and Tencent Video. Unlike matchmaking, casual dating thrives on a critical mass of users at the local level. The more users, the greater the choice set when it comes to initiating the process leading to a match and to an eventual rendezvous.[9]

Online dating platforms have revolutionized how people meet. In the United States, meeting online is now the most frequent way in which heterosexual couples first meet—at a whopping 30%—displacing friends, which used to occupy the number one spot. Every other way of meeting your other half (work, school, family, church, or neighbors) has declined over the past two decades, with the only exception of bars or restaurants. For same-sex couples, online is now the dominant method of meeting—more than 70% of the time. Moreover, research indicates relationship satisfaction is only marginally higher when couples met at primary or secondary school or at a place of worship, for instance. And there is no measurable difference in breakup rates between online and offline couples, with the only exception of having met through friends—which actually *increases* breakup rates.[10]

Given the nature of dating as an activity that involves both personal and social aspects, it should come as no surprise that the market is highly segmented, even within a given country. Moreover, people of different ages and backgrounds prefer to use platforms where they can meet other people like themselves.

In the United States, apps such as Tinder, Ashley Madison, AdultFriendFinder, and C-date compete in the area of casual dating, while Elite Singles and eHarmony fight it out in matchmaking. Users can find online romantic dating platforms like Chemistry, Zoosk, Plenty of Fish, and OKCupid. A similar proliferation of platforms has occurred in China and Europe. Platforms tend not to be independent players. Large, publicly listed companies operate several platforms: Match Group (Tinder, Ourtime, Match, Meetic, Hinge, OKCupid, Plenty of Fish) and the Meet Group (Tagged, Lovoo, MeetMe) dominate the field.

In terms of the international expansion of dating platforms, Tinder is not the most popular app throughout the world, a direct result of the fact that the network effects are primarily local. It is the market leader in the United States, Canada, the United Kingdom, Ireland, France, Belgium, Holland, Scandinavia, Israel, India, the Philippines, Singapore, Australia, and New Zealand. Badoo is the leader in most Latin American, southern and eastern European, and Middle Eastern markets. Lovoo has the upper hand in German-speaking central Europe. Other markets have their own market leader: Russia (Frim), China (Momo), Taiwan (iPair Meet Your Match), Vietnam (Paktor), Japan (YCC), South Korea (Heartbeep), and Saudi Arabia (WhosHere). This proliferation of local players is driven not only by the personal and social nature of casual dating but also by the local nature of the network effects.

In spite of its profitability, a platform like Tinder faces a key strategic challenge: the need to confront a different set of competitors in nearly every country. While the network effects are local, platforms in this space tend to be positioned at the national level, incorporating cultural features and peculiarities. Like many other social platforms with a captive audience of users, Tinder has the potential of diversifying in many different directions, including ecommerce, e-health, wellness, social networking beyond dating, event reservations, food delivery, travel, gyms, and so on, although it has not yet pursued any of these opportunities.

The staying power of dating platforms became readily apparent during the pandemic, which did reduce growth in terms of new users and willingness to pay, but led to a sudden increase in engagement by existing users. Tinder's reluctance to pivot toward video dating meant losing ground relative to competitors like Bumble and Facebook Dating, which are moving much faster to embrace virtual relationships. Even Hinge and Plenty of Fish, dating platforms owned by the same corporate parent as Tinder, have been quicker to join the trend.

Local Network Effects: Uber's Regulatory Strategy

Uber is the best-known digital platform in the world, so much so that the *Collins English Dictionary* now includes an entry for the verb "uberize": "to subject (an industry) to a business model in which services are offered on demand through direct contact between a customer and a supplier, usually via mobile technology."[11]

But this fame is a double-edged sword. *Collins* is now considering adding the term "uberization," or "the conversion of existing jobs and services into discrete tasks that can be requested on-demand; the adoption of the business model used by the taxi service Uber."[12] For many people, the word "uberization" carries a negative connotation. It is a platform that has put many people out of business, developed an organizational culture that is unable to contain harassment, and defied governments in its quest for global domination.

The tension between the good and the bad, the creative and the destructive, lies at the core of Uber as a digital platform. Uber operates in 850 cities located in 80 countries. However, there are 4,500 cities in the world with more than 100,000 residents. In many of the larger ones, Uber attempted to establish a critical mass of drivers and riders but eventually lost to a local competitor—such as Didi in China, Ola in India, Grab in Southeast Asia, Easy Taxi in Latin America, Cabify or mytaxi in Europe, or Mondo in sub-Saharan Africa.

Once again, we see that local network effects result in a proliferation of platforms, each with a strong critical mass in the local market.

Despite its might, the main reason Uber has failed to become a truly global platform is that the network effects in ride hailing are purely local. Success in one city does not guarantee success in another. The critical mass of drivers on one side and riders on the other must be replicated in every location. Interestingly, it was precisely the local nature of the network effects that enabled Uber to implement the most controversial aspect of its business model: ignoring regulators.

Uber's regulatory strategy has been dubbed "Too Big to Fail." In this strategy, the network effects generated two extremely important dynamics. For starters, being the first company to reach a critical mass of drivers and riders in a given location can potentially pay huge dividends. And second, regardless of the reason, being unsuccessful in one location does not affect success in another location. In addition, in most parts of the world, regulation of taxi services in urban areas is a prerogative of local governments, not national ones. Thus, alienating or angering one municipality does not necessarily result in the same outcome in another locality nearby.

Accordingly, Uber's strategy was to grow as fast as possible while its novel business model remained unregulated, in the hope that becoming big would inoculate the company from regulatory action. It bet the farm on the prediction that both drivers and riders would come to the rescue, thus neutralizing any cease and desist regulatory orders. And given the local nature of the network effects, if the strategy failed in one city, growth could continue in others.

Uber cofounder, and at the time CEO, Travis Kalanick put it in disarmingly simple terms in an interview with the *Wall Street Journal* in 2013, at the height of the controversies involving the company:[13]

wsj: Did you ever cease?
KALANICK: No.
wsj: Did you ever desist?
KALANICK: No.
wsj: So you basically ignored them?

KALANICK: The thing is, a cease and desist is something that says, "Hey, I think you should stop," and we're saying, "We don't think we should."

Let's use the city of London as an illustration of Uber's strategy. The company started operations in early 2012 with the goal of having the platform up and running by the time of the Summer Olympics. London was Uber's 11th major-city operation at the time. By the end of 2019, the platform had attracted 40,000 drivers and 3.5 million regular riders. The competitive landscape was complex, but not daunting. It included black cabs, minicabs, private-hire operators, and ride-hailing apps like Hailo. The cabbies lost market share gradually over time and lobbied the municipal government with increasing success.

In September 2017, Transport for London announced it would not renew Uber's operating license. Within a few days, the company organized a petition signed by 800,000 people. In addition, Uber came up with a series of "olive branches," including a 24/7 helpline to handle complaints and criminal activity, a clean air fee to help drivers upgrade to electric cars, and a willingness to increase fares in central London to help pay for a new congestion charge. It even offered authorities operational data to help with traffic planning. In October, the company formally appealed the decision.

Uber continued to operate in London until November 2019, when the city revoked the license on the grounds of continuing rider-safety incidents. The company appealed and continued to operate throughout COVID-19 lockdowns. Although the stay-at-home orders caused its original business to decline sharply, its Uber Eats delivery service boomed. Thus far, it has indeed been "too big to ban" in London.

National Network Effects: The Growth of Monster—and How LinkedIn Stole the Show

Monster.com is a two-sided platform on which companies and job seekers connect and obtain career advice. Its origins go back to the mid-1990s, when the internet was starting to grow. Jeff Taylor's idea was simple but powerful: make newspaper job postings available on a searchable digital board. Not surprisingly, millions of companies and job seekers flocked to the platform, making it one of the earliest commercial successes of the digital age. Moreover, by listing jobs advertised in myriad local newspapers, it created a national job platform. Before long, companies started to see the value of advertising directly on Monster. The Monster Board went public in 1996, within a mere two years of launching, and merged with Online Career Center to form Monster.com in 1999.[14]

Taylor's original idea was to create not just a job board but a platform on which people would continue to engage with one another and with companies, even when they were not looking for a job. This vision was truly revolutionary and prescient, as it predated the rise of social networks.

When LinkedIn launched in 2003, Monster tried to play catch-up, but it was too late, and it made the mistake of asking people to pay a membership fee. The "job board" business model was an antiquated way of thinking about the labor market from the start, in the sense that it did not fully leverage the value of the data that companies and job seekers placed on the platform.

The "social network" business model is based on profiles as opposed to résumés, and it enables not just job postings or career services but advertising and user interaction too. LinkedIn provides individual users and companies with networking opportunities well beyond what a job board could offer. When it comes to job searches, it makes it possible for job seekers to contact someone they know at the company in which they are interested. Conversely, LinkedIn enables companies to look at users' professional profiles even when they are not advertising a position.

Although Monster was built on the basis of aggregating and attracting job postings at the national level, it expanded around the world to more than 20 countries by 2002, with a multilocal presence to account for variations in language, best practices when approaching companies, and labor regulations. Operations were essentially country focused. It is worth noting that other competitors, such as Craigslist, created job platforms that operated only at the local level.

LinkedIn, by contrast, started building its network in a completely different way. Instead of compartmentalizing users by locality or by country, it enabled both companies and people to use the platform on a local, national, regional, or global basis, depending on their specific needs and preferences. Thus, a biotech start-up or a physician may wish to participate in a global professional network to source ideas and knowledge from all over the world. By contrast, other companies and individuals may prefer to restrict their networks to specific geographies. Once LinkedIn had accumulated a critical mass of profiles, employers followed suit by promoting their jobs, a two-sided growth sequence that was the precise opposite of what Monster's had been.

Monster's market was invaded by newcomers like Indeed, which launched a different business model in which companies paid per click as opposed to per posting. Thus, Monster tends to attract employers that need to hire a large number of employees. In fact, individual users have complained for years about spam, as companies seek to advertise their openings among as many Monster users as possible. Meanwhile, Indeed remains focused on aggregating job postings from other job boards and from the websites of the companies themselves, thus becoming the go-to website for job searches.

In 2016, Monster was acquired for $429 million by Randstad, the world's second-largest human-resource services firm with walk-in recruitment centers in 40 countries. LinkedIn was purchased by Microsoft for a whopping $26 billion. At the time, Monster was profitable, while LinkedIn was not. More recently, however, Monster has seen its revenue fall, while LinkedIn's continues to grow. By 2019, LinkedIn was at the top of the global online job advertising ranking by revenue, and Monster had fallen to number eight.[15]

Unlike Monster, the geographical scope of LinkedIn is defined by the reach of the social network of an individual user or company. Individual users and companies can build their own networks and determine the scope of their interactions on the platform. The result is that for certain occupations and for certain types of jobs, the network effects may be more local or national than regional or global.

The LinkedIn business model provides individual users and companies with far more flexibility than do local platforms like Craigslist or multinational ones like Monster. In the end, that is the key competitive advantage of a jobs and careers platform based on social networks. Individual users and companies see in it a platform that serves their needs to be professionally connected, give and receive referrals, assess how the labor market is changing, look for a job, and obtain valuable knowledge and advice at any and all geographical levels.

Regional and Global Network Effects: Service Differentiation in the International Remittance Business

Almost by definition, any platform dedicated to the needs of immigrants is international in nature. The immigrant population is large, amounting to 240 million worldwide, with an additional 26 million international refugees.

Perhaps the international service most frequently used by immigrants involves money transfers to family and friends back in their country of origin. Those payments, called remittances, constitute a $600 billion business annually, greater than the amount of either long-term or short-term capital flows to developing countries. The main recipients of remittances are India, China, the Philippines, Mexico, and Nigeria. Combined, they account for over one-third of the total dollar value.[16]

Until recently, the field was dominated by traditional banks and specialized money-transfer organizations like Western Union. These services tended to charge high commissions, and it took many hours or even days for the money to reach its destination. Digital remittance platforms have revolutionized the field by cutting both fees and delivery times. According to a World Bank survey, the average cost of sending money back to family or friends was 10.2% for banks,

7.7% for money-transfer organizations, 6.2% for digital platforms, and 5.5% for the postal service. Costs are highest in sub-Saharan Africa and lowest in South Asia. In spite of the higher costs, banks still enjoy a 20% global market share of the remittances market. For large amounts or for international transfers between banks, many immigrants prefer to pay the higher fees for peace of mind.[17]

Given that nearly half of all international migration in the world is regional—Africans who migrate from one African country to another, for example—and that the other half of international migration is interregional, the network effects on remittance platforms are a mix of regional and global. In addition, international immigration is skewed toward a few large countries and regions, including China, India, Southeast Asia, Mexico, and South America as the most important origins, and the United States and Europe as the two largest destinations. These two features, combined with the nature of the origin and destination of the money itself (such as a bank account, wiring service, or mobile phone), have resulted in a considerable degree of differentiation among the largest competitors.

Among digital platforms, TransferWise is the largest in volume. It specializes in bank-to-bank transfers. Ria Money Transfer has grown among Spanish-speaking immigrants in North America and Spain. Some platforms have grown on the basis of network effects within the region of origin (WorldRemit, tilted toward immigrants from Africa), or within the destination region (Azimo, focused on immigrants in Europe). Thus, the digital remittance business is not dominated by one large player leveraging global network effects.

If start-up platforms like Tinder, Uber, LinkedIn, and the various remittance services can leverage local, national, regional, and global effects—depending on the circumstances and the nature of their business—can established companies adopt a similar approach to fend off disruption and accelerate their growth?

The biggest incumbent in the remittance market is Western Union, which in addition to its digital capabilities has a large network of physical stores and agencies around the world. It still holds the lion's share of the worldwide remittance business. The company's origins date back to the mid-nineteenth century, during the early years of the telegraph era. In addition to its online and mobile money transfer platforms, the company collaborates with social media and chatting platforms. The next chapter provides further analysis and examples.

The Platform Paradox: Things to Remember

- Network effects
  - shape the way in which digital platforms create value, grow internationally, and deal with regulators.
  - are the demand-side equivalent of economies of scale, which have to do with the supply side of producing a good or service.
- Network effects and economies of scale are synergistic. Network effects attract users, whereas economies of scale reduce average costs as the user base grows, which in turn attracts more users.
- Network effects are also synergistic with switching costs. The greater the network effect, the greater the cost of losing one's contacts when switching from one platform to another.
- Network effects come in many shapes and forms, including dyadic/multiparty, unidirectional/bidirectional/ multidirectional, and one-/two-sided. In two-sided platforms, strategic cross subsidization and price discrimination are the main competitive tools.
- The analysis of the geographical scope of network effects— local, national, regional, or global—lies at the core of the strategy of international expansion in terms of sequence, speed, and mode.

Chapter 3

The Digital Transformation
of Traditional Businesses

The story is among the most familiar in the world of business. Once upon a time, people had hourglasses, clocks, or pocket watches to order, monitor, and sequence daily activities—or they relied on the local church bells. It occurred to someone in Switzerland that wearing a compact watch around the wrist was extremely convenient. The British had dominated the watchmaking industry, but the Swiss persevered, specialized, and innovated, eventually becoming the leading watchmakers to the world. Watches were made in small batches, and they were expensive. The Swiss maintained their leadership during the two world wars. Rolex was one of several firms that reigned supreme.

But US watchmakers realized that there was a market for cheap timepieces made with alloy metals instead of precious metals, friction-resistant cogs instead of jewels, and batteries instead of springs. Timex became the world's largest and most profitable watchmaker by mass producing low-cost wristwatches. Swiss engineers continued to innovate, coming up with the tuning fork as a simpler and more precise mechanism to measure time. But Alpine companies refused to change their ways. It was Bulova, a US firm, that capitalized on the superiority of the tuning fork.

Then came quartz, another technology invented in Switzerland. Japanese companies like Seiko and Citizen came to dominate the global market, thanks to this new technology. By the time the post–World War II boom was over in the wake of the oil crisis, another

Japanese firm, Casio, had incorporated integrated circuits and digital readouts into wristwatches. The digitization of the wristwatch had just begun in earnest. A few years later, the Swiss reclaimed their global leadership position by making colorful, collectible wristwatches under the Swatch brand, turning the device into a fashion accessory.

The most threatening disruption of the watchmaking industry occurred at the turn of the twenty-first century, when computer and electronics companies realized the potential of a minicomputer worn around the wrist. When Apple introduced its revolutionary smartwatch in 2015, mass-market watch companies were put on notice. A product substitute with tremendous capabilities and value-creation potential could seriously threaten their very existence, in a manner similar to when the telephone replaced the telegraph, the transistor bettered the vacuum tube, the word processor did away with the typewriter, or digital photography put an end to its chemical predecessor. Since the 1980s, American and Japanese watch companies have invested millions in developing smartwatches, but it was very difficult to create a useful and exciting ecosystem around the device itself. Apple and Samsung became the world's largest smartwatch companies, as well as the largest smartphone brands.

Traditional businesses across the entire economy continue to scramble to find a pivot in the digital age. They have been affected in different ways by the rise of digital platforms. Some have seen their entire business model undermined, from brick-and-mortar retailers to printed newspapers, and from taxicabs to hotels. Others have managed to survive in a niche market, as in the case of vinyl music records. Intermediaries have been badly hit, such as those in tourism and financial services. The education and healthcare sectors, among the biggest in the economy, have digitized their back offices and operations, though without shifting away from their traditional mode of delivery, except in the wake of the coronavirus pandemic. Companies have invested huge amounts of human and financial resources to reconfigure each activity along the value chain, from their sources of supply to the end consumer.

I will illustrate the dynamics behind success and failure in the digital transformation of traditional businesses with a variety of companies from different industries and countries. The case of Zara, the world's largest apparel retailer, represents the successful incorporation of digital platforms into an omnichannel strategy. Walmart offers a more protracted path to transformation in the case of a company that is not vertically integrated and operates under as many as 55 different banners. The New York Times Company is an example of a firm beleaguered by the digital revolution that has managed to deliver its product digitally alongside the traditional printed format. By contrast, ebooks have not yet captured the imagination of consumers, an outcome similar to wine selling, which remains largely offline in most markets around the world, with only a handful of exceptions. Finally, the legendary toy company Lego has weathered the onslaught of video games, in part by unleashing the power of digital platforms for online sales and crowdsourcing.

Zara: Digital "Fast Fashion"

As the world's biggest apparel retailer, Inditex—the parent company of Zara—is no newcomer to online sales. The company has grown to prominence thanks to its "fast fashion" concept, whereby "fresh" and "perishable" fashion is retailed in stores built on the concept of the supermarket.

Vertical integration and shortened production cycles enable the company to respond in near-real time to changing fashion trends and rotate its collections every three weeks. Customers are incentivized to visit the store frequently, before the items run out or are replaced. The average Zara customer visits a store 17 times a year, compared with three or four times for the competition. Zara offers 11,000 articles each season, compared with the 3,000 to 4,000 articles of its competitors. To maximize sales, the company developed a system to calculate precise quantities of merchandise in each of its nearly 7,500 stores across a portfolio of brands located in 96 countries and territories. The company sources from Spain, eastern Europe, northern Africa, and East Asia and can deliver from its centralized logistics hub to its European stores within 36 hours—and within 48 hours to the rest of the world.[18]

Global online sales of apparel and footwear grow at 25% annual rates, followed at a distance by vending at around 6%. The online channel generates value for the customer in the form of lower prices, convenience, access to a wider range of products, availability of sizes and styles, and algorithmic-driven recommendations. The 2019 Lifestyle Survey by Euromonitor International found that the most important factors in online fashion sales were price (43% of global responders), 24/7 convenience (38%), free shipping (37%), range of brands (30%), lack of availability in local stores (29%), ease of shipping and delivery (28%), information, price, and quality comparison (27%), and instantaneous purchase (24%).[19]

Given this constellation of responses, the online channel can be both a blessing and a curse for established fashion retailers. It can enhance customer value, but at the cost of thinner margins and reduced brand loyalty, given how easy it is to compare prices, qualities, and availability online. For apparel companies, the advantages of the online channel lie in easier order tracking, better inventory management, asset optimization, and direct customer feedback not only from purchases but also from searches and comparisons. But the winning strategy seems to be an omnichannel strategy aimed at obtaining synergies, as opposed to a mere multichannel strategy including stores, department store corners, catalog sales, telephone sales, online store, mobile app, and social media.

Inditex initiated its online strategy in 2007 with its Zara Home brand, which did not have as extensive a retail network of stores as Zara. Given the logistics and fulfillment constraints, it launched in 13 European markets. After some experience, it went ahead and made Zara apparel available online in 16 European markets, which at the time had the largest density of physical stores. The following year, the company added some of its other brands to its online channel in Europe (Pull & Bear, Bershka, Massimo Dutti, Stradivarius, Oysho, and Uterqüe). It also went digital with Zara in the United States and

Japan, markets in which its physical presence was much less dense than in Europe. In 2012, the company launched Zara online in China. Zara's China strategy accelerated in 2014 with an alliance with Alibaba and Tmall. Meanwhile, other brands were made available online in the United States, Canada, Australia, and Japan. By 2016, the company had a full online presence in all European Union markets, Turkey, China, Japan, South Korea, and others.[20]

Given the concept of fast fashion, Inditex decided to accelerate order fulfillment. In 2017 it offered a same-day guarantee in Madrid, London, Paris, Istanbul, Taipei, and Shanghai, and next-day in all of Spain, France, the UK, Poland, China, and South Korea. In the following years the company added new cities, including New York, Mexico City, Warsaw, Sydney, Moscow, and Toronto. This required investing in 16 last-mile logistics hubs specifically tasked with online sales. By the end of 2019, online sales represented 14% of total sales in markets in which the company had online sales, and 100% in dozens of markets in which it lacked physical stores.

When it comes to fashion, social platforms are a key component of online strategy. In Zara's case, it is even more so because of the brand's strategy of not engaging in promotional marketing or traditional advertising. It spends a mere 0.3% of sales on advertising, but has amassed over 30 million Instagram followers and 28 million Facebook fans by investing in high-quality online content. The overall brand portfolio boasts about 150 million social media followers.

One important aspect of Zara's presence in social media platforms is that it has largely followed a global approach, building its brand image irrespective of cross-national differences. Therefore, the company leverages global network effects. If the point of a social media strategy is to generate hype for the brand and to showcase broad aspects of upcoming collections, it makes sense to maximize the global effects, especially in the context of an omnichannel strategy. The social media channel builds on global network effects, feeding customers to national websites or apps where orders are placed and fulfilled using regional logistics platforms (Europe, North America, East Asia, etc.), or perhaps collected at local stores.

Having said that, online sales have forced Zara to adopt more of a country-by-country, and even city-by-city, strategy when it comes to the downstream activities along the value chain. Online shoppers don't go to the store, except for pickups or exchanges. Fulfilling online orders is a local game that requires either building new capabilities or entering into alliances with local platforms.

In China, a vast and rapidly growing market where Zara has fewer than 200 stores, the brand decided to establish a presence on the Tmall marketplace and enter into a partnership with JD.com (a platform majority owned by Tencent) for one-day delivery. In India, where it has established fewer than 25 stores since it first entered in 2010 in partnership with Tata, the company has not yet made a decision as to how to grow online sales. Tata announced the end of the arrangement, leaving Inditex with no clear strategy, but with more degrees of freedom as to its next move in a consumer market that is poised to become as big as China's within a couple of decades.

Inditex's response to the pandemic focused on making wearable personal protective equipment for hospital workers, worth half a billion dollars, and allocating more resources to online sales. The company was forced to write off about $300 million in unsold inventory. Online sales soared by more than 70% during the lockdown phase, and they continued to be strong during reopening, given social distancing guidelines. But this was not enough. Total sales dropped by 44% during the first quarter of 2020. The company announced the closing of up to 1,200 stores, mostly small outlets that do not fit its omnichannel strategy anyway. It aims to increase online sales to 25% of total sales by 2022.

Walmart's Challenging Digital Growth

"The global consumer is changing," and "one size doesn't fit all," says Judith McKenna, the CEO of Walmart International, a company with an extensive global footprint. As of the end of 2019, the company operated under 55 banners in 26 countries on four continents. It has mainly entered these markets via acquisition or joint venture, having abandoned several key markets after years of losses, including Canada, Brazil, and the UK. Technology is the new name of the game, from inbound logistics to sales and order fulfillment.[21]

In China, where online platform-to-consumer food delivery is growing in excess of 40% per year and has already attracted 300 million consumers, according to Statista,[22] Walmart found that it could not succeed by itself. In 2016 it acquired a 12% stake in JD.com, the Tencent-controlled platform that is assisting Zara with one-day deliveries. Tencent, JD, and Walmart are pooling customer data for mutual advantage. Similarly, in 2018 Walmart acquired Flipkart in India for a hefty $16 billion, a market in which foreign store chains face limitations in opening new locations. In Canada, home to one of Walmart's most abject failures, the company signed an agreement with marketplace Shopify in 2020 to enable third-party sellers to sell on Walmart's website.

Walmart's emerging digital strategy is two-pronged. On the one hand, it seeks to leverage its enormous capabilities in data-driven supply chain management, warehousing, and fulfillment. On the other, it is attempting to ward off the challenges from companies such as Amazon and Alibaba, which have identified food items, and especially fresh produce, as an attractive area for growth. Unlike Zara, however, Walmart is not vertically integrated, meaning that it generates value from inbound and outbound logistics alone, as opposed to generating value from design and manufacturing. Protecting its relationships and position among suppliers is key to its success.

The *New York Times* in the Post-Gutenberg Era

Perhaps no industry has been as severely affected by new technology as printed news media, the industry made possible by Johannes Gutenberg's invention of the modern printing press. The traditional newspaper business model was based on a centralized hub to create content delivered on a daily basis to readers through a capital-intensive printing and physical-distribution system. Revenue came from unit sales, subscriptions, and advertising. While economies of scale certainly played a big role, local newspapers proliferated as well, catering to local audiences and advertisers, which frequently took the form of a classifieds section. Intriguingly, the old model did not make it easy for dailies to have a truly global audience, given transportation costs or the prohibitive investments or alliances required to print a newspaper in several locations around the world.

The post-Gutenberg newspaper landscape bears little resemblance to the old model. Content creation has shifted thanks to crowdsourcing, the rise of "citizen journalists," content aggregation, and more. Less emphasis on printing and physical distribution has created a round-the-clock news cycle in which people expect to be informed 24/7.[23]

Traditional sources of revenue have evaporated as free online news sources undermined unit sales and subscriptions, competition from digital billboards eroded classifieds revenue, and social media advertising displaced the traditional media outlets, whether printed or digital. Newspaper circulation in the United States peaked in the late 1980s at about 65 million copies, declining to just above 30 million copies in the late 2010s. As a result, scores of typographers, press operators, machinists, electricians, mailers, drivers, and paper handlers lost unionized jobs. Revenue from advertising (digital and print) plummeted from a peak of $50 billion in 2008 to about $10 billion by 2019. Digital advertising on newspaper platforms grew from 18% in 2011 to 34% in 2018, not enough to offset the declines in print advertising and circulation revenue. Meanwhile, Google and Facebook grabbed nearly 60% of the national digital advertising market and 77% of the local market.[24]

Newspapers have experimented with a variety of digital revenue models, including ad-based free use, freemium, soft (metered) paywalls, and hard paywalls. The *New York Times* and *Wall Street Journal* are two that have been among the most successful in terms of adapting to the digital age.[25] Both decided to invest heavily in high-quality, original journalism, delivered via website, through an app, and in print. An integral part of this strategy is to promote traffic to the online platforms and attract advertisers. At the same time, converting free users into freemium users and digital subscribers became the best way to establish a solid digital base that contributes to the financial stability of the newspaper.

The *Wall Street Journal* has typically managed a 4.5% conversion rate, and the *New York Times* about 3.5%, leaving behind the *Washington Post* (1.7%), *Chicago Tribune* (0.6%), and the *Dallas Morning News* (0.4%). Gannett, which publishes over two dozen local newspapers as well as *USA Today*, has attained only a 0.5% conversion rate.[26]

The *New York Times* has had more digital than print pay subscribers since 2015, four years after it added its first paywall, which required readers to subscribe after reading 20 articles per month. The *Times* also launched complementary digital products, including the Cooking app and the Crossword app, which account for one-quarter of all digital growth.

But digital advertising has not grown fast enough to offset the decline in print advertising. Whereas in 2000 the newspaper derived 71% of its revenue from advertising (nearly all in print), by 2019 it generated only 29%. Meanwhile, subscription revenue, especially for the digital edition, grew by leaps and bounds. Still, for every dollar of digital subscription revenue, the company collected $1.46 from print subscribers. Advertising revenue was evenly split between digital and print. In terms of total revenue, print was still 30% higher than digital, with the difference declining over time.

The pandemic has exacerbated the trends of plummeting advertising revenue and greater numbers of digital subscribers eager to read news and analysis about the crisis, with over a million new digital subscribers since the beginning of the outbreak, helping the company surpass the 6 million mark. During the third quarter of 2020, the newspaper brought in more revenue from online readers than from print subscribers. Meanwhile, both print and digital advertising revenue shrunk because of the recession, highlighting the growing advantage that platforms such as Facebook and Google enjoy. The digital transformation of the *New York Times* has a long way to go as it seeks to consolidate itself as the leading subscription-based source of quality news and analysis.

The digital edition of the *Times*, offered through the website and as a smartphone app, has enabled the company to expand the scope of its network effects from the national to the global levels in a cost-effective way. The international edition of the *Times* is printed in the English language at 38 facilities throughout the world and distributed in more than 160 countries and territories. Known as the *International Herald Tribune* since 1967, it was a collaborative arrangement with the *Washington Post* and the owners of the original *Paris Herald Tribune*, the Whitney family. By 1991, it had become a joint venture between the *Times* and the *Post*, which lasted until 2002. After several name changes, it became the *New York Times International Edition*, with some columnists of its own. The digital properties were merged into one, with three language versions: English, Spanish, and Simplified Mandarin.

Other major international newspapers have taken a different path toward digitalization and internationalization. The *Guardian*, the British daily founded in 1821, now offers digital US, Australia, and international editions in addition to its printed and digital UK edition. Besides subscription revenue, it has pioneered direct contributions from readers "to deliver the independent journalism the world needs." It offers three tiers of membership: friend (free), supporter, and partner (includes tickets and/or priority booking for online live events and master classes).

The New York Times Company has capitalized on the popularity of its crosswords and cooking recipes to acquire more subscribers and increase revenue. Dow Jones, the parent company of the *Wall Street Journal*, has managed to increase margins even though the paper has a smaller subscriber base; it has done this by bundling its newswires and business information platforms, which are delivered digitally to the user. Thus, the *Times* continues to be more reliant on print than the *Journal*.

Newspapers, and the news media more broadly, continue to struggle in the midst of the digital revolution. The polarization of politics has created an opportunity for high-quality journalism, especially that of the investigative kind. The winning business model seems to include three key ingredients: reader engagement with a differentiated product based on original content, a combination of print and digital editions, and tiered paywalls.

It is remarkable that some of the big names in the newspaper business have survived, and even thrived, in the midst of so much disruption and increased competition from social media, search engines, news aggregators, and other types of digital platforms. Meanwhile, thousands of local newspapers have gone bust around the world, and the survivors have had to engage in deep cuts in staffing and other areas.

eBooks Take a Different Path

In contrast to the newspaper business, the book trade has remained surprisingly traditional. Sales of ebooks have stagnated or even declined, while those of printed books continue to do well. The bound, printed book is a delightful invention. It is intuitive to use, is easy to share, serves as decoration on a shelf—and is quite cheap considering the amount of entertainment it provides.

The advantages of ebooks are equally noteworthy: Tablets make them easy to use, they are eminently easy to search, they do not take up space in the home or the library, they may be carried effortlessly while traveling, and they are even cheaper than printed books. In some areas of publishing, digital formats and platforms have displaced the printed format for good. For instance, nobody buys multivolume encyclopedias anymore; their online versions are much easier to use—and Wikipedia is also available as a crowdsourced alternative to the traditional concept of a universal repository of all knowledge. Scientific publishing has gone almost completely online. Digital educational publishing has grown quickly given that online learning platforms can easily accommodate ebooks as one source of knowledge in addition to others, like podcasts and videos.

Given the comparative balance of pros and cons for printed and digital books, how is it that, when it comes to fiction and nonfiction publishing, the printed version continues to have more demand? For instance, in the United States, the largest publishing market in the world, sales of ebooks peaked in 2014 at 26% of the total value, declining to 14% in 2019. While ebook sales grew more rapidly than printed book sales during the early months of the pandemic, by the summer of 2020 the traditional format had staged a comeback.[27] Meanwhile, audiobooks have gained in market share, reaching 8%, thanks to audio downloads.

Here, the digital revolution has not displaced the old, printed format. But it has certainly changed the way in which printed books and ebooks are sold, with online sales on Amazon alone accounting for half of the US printed book sales and three-quarters of the ebook segment.

Age and generations don't appear to be a factor either. According to the Pew Research Center, millennials report reading more books than any other age group across all formats.[28]

To truly understand why people of all ages prefer the traditional printed format, let's examine why people buy books in the first place. A good starting point is to assume that buyers want to read the book. Research indicates people absorb information more efficiently when they read a printed book than when they read a digital book in an e-reader or tablet.[29] In addition, a printed book allows the reader to easily assess how much of it remains to be read in a very intuitive way—by marking the last page read and looking at the text block to see what fraction of the book's total thickness lies before or after.

Owning a physical book can also be a source of pride, and perhaps that's why so many avid readers mark their books with an "ex libris" or bookplate. People may also want to share the book with family or friends after reading it. Not only are printed books easier to share (at short distances) than digital books, owing to the multiple and incompatible platforms for digital books available in the market, but also passing your own copy of a book onto someone else in your social circle is a form of sharing that can be infused with meaning. The physical object becomes a symbol of friendship or respect.

An article in *Scientific American* argues that reading a book on a screen precludes serendipity. When people read a book, they enjoy flipping back and forth as they make their way through it. And printed books are ideal gifts.[30] In fact, one-third of book sales in the United States year-round come from books that are given as gifts, a proportion that approaches 80% during the holiday season. While people have shunned printed newspapers, most still prefer to gift printed books, wrapped in colorful paper, perhaps with other objects that convey affection.

That said, it is quite likely ebooks will triumph in parts of the world where physical distribution of printed books is impractical or prohibitively expensive. In my 2020 book, *2030: How Today's Biggest Trends Will Collide and Change the Future of Everything*, I argue that ebooks will triumph in Africa, where 450 million babies will be born over the next decade. Educating them will require using technology, in the same way that mobile payments and telemedicine became big trends in Africa before they caught on in other parts of the world. Worldreader, a San Francisco–based nonprofit, provides a free library of digital books for schools throughout the developing world. For rural areas without a connection to the digital network, the company designed an integrated system of solar panels, USB hubs, LED lighting, and e-readers so that people can access ebooks and other learning materials.

Failed Channel Digitalization: Wine

Only a small proportion of total wine sales off-trade (outside bars and restaurants) take place online: 2% of total volume in Italy and Spain; 4% in Germany, Japan, and the United States; and 5% in France, for example. The global average is a paltry 7%, and only three countries have a percentage greater than 10%: China (29%), the UK (11%), and Australia (10%).[31]

Why is it that most consumers reject purchasing wine online? At first sight, it seems irrational that they would purchase more than half of their clothes and footwear online—which need to fit their bodies—but less than 10% of wine, which generally cannot be tasted in the store. Perhaps consumers like to get guidance from the staff at specialized liquor stores. However, only 22% of global sales take place in such a channel; most people purchase their wine at supermarkets, hypermarkets, and discounters. It is also possible that people fear that the bottle might break during shipping, but they nonetheless buy more than half of expensive and fragile items like electronics online. Perhaps wine lovers are impulse buyers, or they realize at the last minute they need to bring a bottle of wine to a party or special occasion.

While those factors certainly limit online wine sales, they fail to explain why China is so ahead of the rest of the world. One potential explanation is that a sizable middle-class market developed there only in the past three decades, with not enough time to build up a network of physical wine stores. But that does not seem to be the case with automobile dealerships. And how can one possibly explain that the UK and Australia are the only other markets with a sizable online sales volume?

Intriguingly, the answer has to do with the format of the product that consumers prefer to purchase. Unlike books, the key distinction when it comes to wine is obviously not physical versus digital, but *terroir* versus branded. The former has to do with the origin of the wine, while the latter relates to the market. Terroir wine is defined by the specific characteristics of the type of grape, climate, exposure to the sun, type of soil, and cultural and historical influences. Branded wine, by contrast, is defined by a narrative linking the product to a specific segment of the market. While it is true that some terroir wines are sold under a brand name, most are sold under a label that designates it as coming from a specific vineyard and winery. In France, for instance, there are as many as 27,000 wineries, many of them producing multiple kinds of terroir wines.

The point of this distinction is that branded wine lends itself more easily to the online channel. It just so happens that a large middle-class market for wine emerged in China, the UK, and Australia beginning in the late 1980s, albeit for different reasons. In China, that was when the middle class came into being, and the bulk of it preferred the simplicity, uniformity, and appeal of branded wines. In the UK and Australia, beer had been the preferred alcoholic drink for daily consumption. One of the world's best-known wine brands is Australia's Yellow Tail. Julie Bower, an expert on the British market, has pointed out that the growth of the wine market in the UK to become one of the world's largest "owes much to the success of . . . early brands and those that arrived later in the 1990s, with Australia displacing France as the source for mass-market appeal."[32] Thus, online wine sales are greater in countries that developed a large consumer market for wine more recently, and thus are tilted toward branded wines.

Lego: The "Apple of Toys"

Another case in which the channel and the ecosystem are more important than the product format involves Lego. Its bricks have captured the imagination of generations of children and adults alike. The company has been dubbed the "Apple of Toys," but that has not prevented it from going through multiple cycles of boom and bust, and even flirting with bankruptcy. During the 1990s, this family-owned and unlisted company headquartered in a small Danish village was reeling from the success of video games and other types of electronic toys. It decided to reinvent itself as a "lifestyle" company, venturing into Lego-branded clothes, jewelry, and watches. Each of these new ventures eventually failed.[33]

The new chief executive appointed in 2001, Jørgen Vig Knudstorp, saw the opportunity in going "back to the brick." Sales soared to such an extent that Lego became the largest toy company in the world, surpassing Hasbro and Mattel, thanks in part to the use of digital tools. Nearly a million adults are members of its Lego Ideas online community. That's actually the main way the company has incorporated the digital revolution into its business—by engaging users as opposed to changing its product, by relying on the wisdom of crowds, which is also the title of James Surowiecki's best-selling book. "If you want to act in a world that is constantly disrupting," says Lars Silberbauer, Lego's director of social media and video, "you have to have as many different perspectives on what you're doing right now." It's implemented a variant of crowdsourcing to encourage and enable customers and fans to provide the company with information about their needs and wants. "Four new products come out of this program every year, pretty much with no marketing budget because the excitement and engagement have already been built up throughout the crowdsourcing phase."[34]

Lego was founded in 1932 by Ole Christiansen. Manufacturing of its signature plastic bricks with eight studs in two rows of four—called Automatic Binding Bricks—began in 1949. The founder's son, Godtfred, improved on Hilary Fisher Page's Self-Locking Building Bricks and filed for a US patent in 1958 called Toy Building Brick. The basic idea behind it was that of compatibility.

"Before Lego, there really was no system of toys that worked together," writes Will Reed. "The versatility of this system lets the user build just about anything they can dream of: a dinosaur, car, building, even something that only exists in the world of tomorrow."[35] The idea unleashed another important potential. Unlike a jigsaw puzzle, "just six bricks yield more than 915 million potential combinations," writes David Robertson in the book *Brick by Brick: How LEGO Rewrote the Rules of Innovation and Conquered the Global Toy Industry.*[36]

After the product diversification fiasco of the 1990s, Lego refocused but continued to branch out. First came video games, buildable action figures, and board games, and then box-office blockbusters such as *The Lego Movie, The Lego Batman Movie,* and *The Lego Ninjago Movie.* In a way, Lego discovered the recipe for sustainable success was to bridge the gap between generations. "Regardless of age or ability, anyone can pick up Lego pieces and let their imagination run wild," observes John Hanlon, a TV producer who launched the Lego YouTube channel along with his brother Joshua in 2011. "Lego brings together the young and old for wholesome, non-electronic fun."[37]

During the COVID-19 pandemic, sales of board games, jigsaw puzzles, and Legos soared as parents and children were confined to their homes. It helped that the Danish company has a diversified supply chain focused on Mexico and Europe, with almost no dependence on China, and that it was prepared to scale up its online sales.

How to Envision and Implement a Digital Transformation

The cases of Zara, Walmart, the *New York Times*, and Lego show the way toward the digital transformation of traditional businesses. The golden rule is that digital cannot merely be an add-on to the company's preexisting strategic posture. Rather, it needs to be tightly integrated with every operation inside the company and along the value chain reaching backward to suppliers and forward to customers.

Zara succeeded by embracing an omnichannel strategy, albeit much remains to be done given its declining sales during the pandemic. In spite of its logistics prowess, Walmart suffers from a multiplicity of platforms under 55 banners and intense competition in the fresh-produce segment from giants like Amazon. Perhaps the *New York Times* demonstrated that it is possible to persuade digital readers to pay for high-quality content, but it has not yet gone far enough when it comes to implementing a fully digital strategy and still has much work to do if it is to thrive in the digital age. Lego showed that one can be a profitable toy company not by making electronic toys and video games but by learning from the customer through technology and making traditional toys attractive to children and adults alike. It is precisely because the digital transformation of legacy businesses is so slow and difficult that start-ups often triumph.

The multiplying power of the network effects unleashed by digital platforms is unforgiving. Basically, apparel designers and retailers never thought of themselves as being in a network business.

Neither did newspapers or toy companies. Online ecommerce platforms, social media, and collaborative computer gaming changed the rules of the game. Once the genie came out of the bottle, competition shifted toward the strategic use of network effects to obtain growth and profits.

The Platform Paradox: Things to Remember

- Traditional companies face the challenge of building new digital capabilities while defending their turf against disruptors.
- Companies that are vertically integrated (Zara) follow a path toward digital transformation that is different from the path followed by companies that are not vertically integrated (Walmart).
- Other traditional companies, such as the printed media, see their entire business model disrupted. In that case, the entire business model, from content generation to delivery, needs to be overhauled.
- In some businesses, demand characteristics offer ways for the traditional model to survive and even continue to dominate the market, as in the cases of printed books and wine sales.

Chapter 4

The Internationalization
of Digital Platforms

Airbnb, now a global behemoth, got its big break in Washington, DC, in early 2009. One of its founders sensed an opportunity: an acute scarcity of hotel rooms during the inauguration of President Barack Obama.

After months of adjustments and tweaks to its business model, Airbnb expanded to other localities in the United States and Canada. Europe came next, but that's a collection of many different countries and cultures as opposed to a unified one. Entering just a few cities to make sure enough critical mass of hosts existed made sense as an overall strategy. But Europeans prefer to visit a different city each time, and Americans and Asians are similarly inclined.

How should Airbnb build up its international presence? One city at a time or one country at a time? Or should it perhaps think about the nature of network effects and then adapt the sequence of international expansion accordingly? And how about its revenue model? The company's original market position consisted of being an intermediary between guests and hosts. Would it need to change its business model so as to capitalize on other sources of revenue?

International Expansion: The Sequential Model

International expansion in the digital age comes with two big misconceptions. The first is that online companies can enter any national market around the world in a frictionless and effortless way. After all, the internet is a global medium, and companies can offer any product or service to all, no matter where the consumer or user is located. It is arguably true that the digital channel enables companies to potentially reach anyone, anywhere. In the case of tangible goods, the biggest limitation is order fulfillment, given that a proprietary or rented physical infrastructure is needed. For services, the conventional wisdom goes, no such constraints exist.

In reality, even companies that use digital media to sell intangible services such as those offered by many platforms face multiple obstacles:

- Market access restrictions, cultural barriers, unfamiliarity with local market characteristics, technological constraints such as broadband capacity, and so on.
- Lack of awareness on the part of consumers and users. Having an online presence does not automatically result in awareness, let alone interest and purchase.
- Marketing and promotional practices differ from country to country, thus requiring an entry strategy tailored to each market.
- The presence of local competitors—oftentimes mere clones— that know the landscape much better.

The second misconception about business in the digital age is that successful companies can leverage network effects (on the demand side) and economies of scale (on the supply side) to generate overwhelming first-mover advantages in winner-take-all situations, thus becoming globally dominant in their fields. Every digital platform faces local competitors, and some of them have a presence in multiple national markets themselves.

Local network effects, in particular, make it more likely for local competitors to flourish. We saw in chapter 2 that Uber faces different competing platforms depending on the national market (Lyft in the United States, Grab in Southeast Asia, Easy Taxi in Latin America, and Cabify in Europe). Tinder is the market leader in just about a dozen national markets, but the underdog in most Latin American, European, Middle Eastern, and East Asian markets.

Given that international expansion is an obstacle course punctuated by institutional, cultural, linguistic, regulatory, technological, and competitive traps, it makes sense to think about how companies should allocate their scarce resources to overcome them. Entering all markets in the world simultaneously works for very few companies. One might mention the example of Google's search engine, which handles over 90% of the total number of queries worldwide, followed at an abysmal distance by Bing (2.6%), Yahoo! (1.7%), Baidu (1.4%), and Yandex (0.5%), the Russian search engine.[38]

For the immense majority of digital platforms, thinking about international expansion in a *sequential* way is the most likely path to success. The sequential model of international expansion is predicated on three main postulates:

1. International expansion should begin after the company has secured a solid presence in the home country. In the case of digital platforms, this recommendation is only useful when national network effects predominate.
   - If national network effects are very strong, the platform needs to capture a critical mass of users in the national market before any other competitor does. This is especially true in the case of two-sided platforms where one type of users will ignore the platform until there are enough users on the other side (ride hailing, accommodation sharing, dating, ecommerce, etc.).
   - If local network effects are the norm (ride hailing or casual dating), a successful digital platform can establish itself in foreign localities at any moment, assuming it has reached critical mass in each of the localities in which it already has a presence. Otherwise, a local competitor may take the lead in that local market.
   - Note, however, that most companies prefer to reach critical mass quickly in as many local markets in the

home country as possible before venturing abroad because the regulatory, cultural, and technological constraints are less important within than across countries. This principle boils down to going after the low-hanging fruit first in order to build scale before the competition does.

- If regional or global network effects predominate (immigrant remittances or search engines), a digital platform must create critical mass within a short window of opportunity in each region or in the world as a whole, as we will see later in this chapter using Airbnb as an example.

2. International expansion should follow the path of least resistance, prioritizing markets that pose fewer challenges from regulatory, cultural, technological, and competitive points of view. The key to implementing this principle successfully is to adopt the correct definition of the market—namely, local, national, regional, or global—taking into account the nature of the network effects.

3. The speed of international expansion across many markets is a function of how quickly the platform can reach critical mass, reap economies of scale, and fend off competitors in each market, defined at the local, national, regional, or global level.

Airbnb: Business Model, International Presence, and Competitors

Uber operates in 600 cities located in 65 countries. Airbnb offers accommodations in 65,000 locations in 191 countries. Both are two-sided sharing platforms, but they are subject to radically different network effects. Uber's are local. Is Airbnb subject to national, regional, or global effects? To answer that question, let's examine what Airbnb does.

Airbnb has disrupted the traditional hospitality sector by offering an alternative value proposition based on both cost and quality.

Brian Chesky, cofounder and CEO, has emphasized the importance of the experience factor in Airbnb's growth strategy: "I think the key that makes Airbnb is the fact that we're a community, not just a series of commodities." Many guests are drawn to the platform because they are looking for a different way to enjoy travel. "I don't travel to relax, I travel to have new and interesting experiences," says River Tatry, a 23-year-old New York freelancer. "For me, it is much more worthwhile to integrate myself into a place, learn something new, make local friends to visit again, and build community."[39]

The two-sided nature of the platform has enabled it to grow quickly, for several reasons. On the supply side, the following trends are worth noting:

- Supply constraints in large cities with demand peaks during special events or vacation periods.
- Scarcity of offerings in rural areas owing to decades of underinvestment in traditional hospitality outside of metropolitan areas or resort towns.
- A growing generation of empty nesters with space to rent, combined with a greater need to obtain supplemental income to make it through retirement in the age of pension cuts and longer life expectancy, and an epidemic of loneliness.

On the demand side, Airbnb rode several waves of change:

- A younger generation of users looking for an experience when they travel. Millennials account for 60% of bookings in the United States, and over 80% in China.
- Shifting preferences: While 55% use Airbnb to find the best price, one-third are interested in a more authentic experience, access to a kitchen, and/or a unique accommodation that is not the classic hotel room.[40]

The founding team realized that there were two distinct generations—millennials and empty nesters—with complementary assets and wants. The team merely created a two-sided platform so that the two groups could interact with one another. Over the years, Airbnb turned itself into a full-fledged accommodation intermediary as opposed to a sharing platform given that over half of all listings in most local markets are owned and managed by multiunit owners, many of them commercial entities as opposed to individuals or couples.

But Airbnb is not like Google. It's not the only game in town. It does not control 90% of the global market. In the United States it faces stiff competition from HomeAway, Vrbo (Vacation Rentals by Owner), Couchsurfing, and Tripping, among others. Globally, hosts and guests can also use Booking, Casamundo, FlipKey, HomeAway (owned by TripAdvisor), HouseTrip, Kid & Coe, and VacationRentals, among many other platforms. Some platforms are big in specific parts of the world or in specific countries—for example, Agoda Homes, Bookabach, Kid & Coe, Stayz, Travelmore, Alterkeys, Atraveo, Halldis, Holiday Lettings, Niumba, Toprural, and SleepOut.

Some of them have shut down, but others have reached critical mass and pose great threats to Airbnb. Wimdu is the biggest platform for holiday rentals in Europe, the largest tourism market in the world. It is a platform of platforms in the sense that it refers the user to another website or app where the listing was originally made, such as Booking, Expedia, FlipKey, HomeAway, Vrbo, and Airbnb.

Most of these alternative platforms occupy a niche, however, such as vacation rentals for bigger groups, ultra-low price accommodations, or rural tourism. For instance, Tujia is larger than Airbnb in China, but it specializes in intergenerational travel groups.

HomeAway ranks as the second-largest global platform, with over a million worldwide listings, compared with over 5 million on Airbnb, which prides itself on having hundreds of millions of hosts and guests. Still, every year international tourists take 1.4 billion trips to another country, and domestic tourists take nearly 4 billion trips within their countries of residence, according to data from the World Bank and the Organisation for Economic Co-operation and Development.[41]

Airbnb: Sequence of International Expansion

From its humble origins in late 2007 and the launching of its website 10 months later to achieving unicorn status in 2011, Airbnb expanded around the world as follows:

- 2008–2011: experiences organic growth in hosts and guests through word of mouth, first in North America and later in Latin America and Europe.
- May 2011: acquires German clone Accoleo, with offices in Hamburg and Berlin.
- October 2011: opens office in London to promote its platform.
- 2012: opens offices in Paris, Berlin, Hamburg, Milan, Barcelona, Copenhagen, Moscow, São Paulo, and Delhi.
- October 2012: acquires London-based clone CrashPadder.
- 2012: opens offices in Sydney and Singapore (as Asian headquarters). Australia becomes Airbnb's second-largest market by bookings. Additional effort is made in Thailand and Indonesia, among the largest tourism markets in the world.
- 2013: establishes European headquarters in Dublin.
- 2015: announces partnership with Deutsche Telekom (T-Mobile) to have its app preinstalled in mobile phones sold in 13 countries.
- 2015–2019: grows to offer over 5 million listings in 65,000 locations in 191 countries.

Airbnb's success has been based on having ever larger numbers of hosts add their listings. That in turn attracts more users from both the host's country and all other countries in the world, which further encourages more hosts to list. The virtuous circle is in fact the result of a complex web of network effects operating on a global scale. Does this mean that Airbnb should promote its platform to hosts (and guests) no matter where they are in the world, as long as it keeps adding more? Or should the company prioritize in a certain way?

Figure 4.1. National Tourism Markets Prioritized by Size

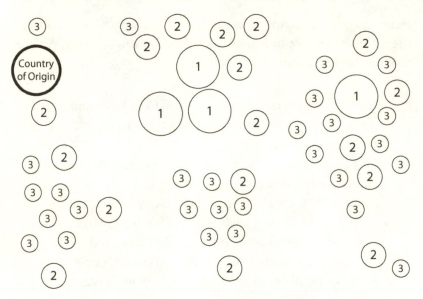

The answer to this question is not simple. In principle, Airbnb runs the risk of spreading itself too thinly across too many countries in the world at the cost of not reaching critical mass in any of them and thus creating an opening for local competitors and clones. As the sequence of events above seems to indicate, the company did in fact prioritize markets, shifting its attention and resources over time. When it comes to prioritizing markets, there are several possibilities.

Figure 4.1 displays one such possibility. It entails entering the markets with the largest potential size first, as measured by the number of tourism arrivals, domestic and international. The first tier of countries to emphasize are those labeled as "1"; these countries include France, Spain, China, and Italy, which are the largest tourism markets in the world in addition to the United States.[42]

After reaching critical mass in those countries, Airbnb could pour resources into tier 2 countries such as Mexico, Turkey, Germany, the UK, Brazil, Japan, Thailand, Australia, South Africa, and Egypt. The problem with this approach is that, for example, a German tourist who books an accommodation in France in a given year may wish

Figure 4.2. National Tourism Markets Prioritized by Cultural Similarity

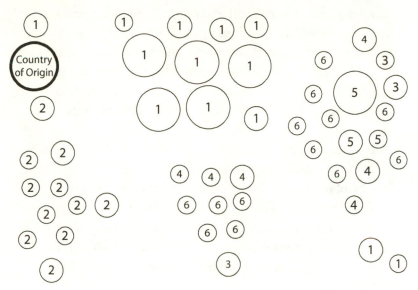

to travel to Greece the following year, a country where Airbnb perhaps has not yet achieved critical mass, or a French tourist who stays at a listing in France may later want to take a vacation in Hungary.

Another possibility many companies entertain when entering foreign markets is to follow a sequence in terms of cultural similarity with a view to ensuring that the service is attractive to potential guests and that hosts feel comfortable listing their properties. In that case, Airbnb should prioritize Canada, Europe, Australia, and New Zealand, followed by Mexico and South America, and then South Korea, Japan, and South Africa, leaving the rest of Asia, the Middle East, and Africa for a later stage (see figure 4.2).

This second criterion, however, raises even more serious issues regarding people's desired travel destinations over time. For instance, an adventurous potential guest who lives in Canada may feel that Airbnb is of limited use if it only has a strong presence in countries that are culturally similar to the United States. Instead of size of the market and cultural similarity, one might establish priorities in terms of average purchasing power, political risk, regulatory similarities, or other features of countries.

To design a better international sequence of expansion, we need to focus on the nature of the network effects that characterize this type of two-sided platform. Tourism, whether for work or for pleasure, falls under three distinct geographical categories: national, regional, and global. In most countries in the world, the lion's share of tourism as measured by person-trips is of national origin:

- In large countries such as the United States, 97% of trips in 2019 were domestic. However, domestic tourism represented 84% of total spending by travelers in the United States. Tourism in China has similar proportions.
- In medium-size countries, like France, Germany, or Spain, domestic tourism is about 75% of total person-trips, and spending by domestic travelers amounts to about 45% of the total.
- In tiny countries like Luxembourg or Singapore, nearly all tourism is international.

It is important to dig further into international tourism. At least three-quarters of it is regional, such as within Europe, Latin America, North America and the Caribbean, Asia, Africa, or the Middle East. Regional travelers spend more nights and more money per trip than domestic tourists, but less than global travelers. Both tourism for pleasure and tourism for work follow similar proportions.

Based on those proportions and relationships, Airbnb's optimal sequence of international expansion as a two-sided platform would be as follows:

1. The strategy's initial aim is to create a critical mass of listings in as many locations as possible within the home country, the United States, given that the overwhelming majority of tourists are *domestic*. Having accommodations available in many locations across the entire country will attract not only

American guests but also those from the rest of the world, thus multiplying the network effects on both sides of the platform.

2. Given that *regional* tourism is the largest share of international tourism, the second step is to reach a critical mass of listings in the region in which the home country is situated (i.e., North America). This prescription is consistent with the fact that nearly half of American international tourists have Canada and Mexico as their destinations, and that travelers from Canada and Mexico represent about half of all international tourists arriving in the United States. Extending the critical mass of listings to all of North America also attracts to Airbnb tourists from the rest of the world who are looking for accommodations not just in the United States but also in Canada and Mexico. As in the first step, this strategy maximizes the potential network effects on both sides of the platform.

3. The third step would be to reach a critical mass of listings in another region, the one with the largest number of tourists to the United States and North America as a whole, and with the largest number of North American international tourists—namely, Europe, which represents about a fifth of total tourism. Note that it is essential to reach critical mass not only in the largest origins of European tourists to North America or the largest destinations of North Americans in Europe (in decreasing order, the UK, Germany, and France), but in all of Europe, given that 75% of European tourism has another European country or location as its destination. This is the only way of ensuring that no European competitor will grow too big before Airbnb builds up its presence. Once again, taking this third step maximizes the network effects on both sides of the platform.

4. The next steps would be to go down the ranking of regions by number of travelers to and from not only the United States but also North America and Europe—namely, East Asia,

followed by South America, South Asia, the Middle East, and Africa. Within each region, critical mass needs to be reached in each country and location before a local competitor becomes too big.

5. If a local competitor has already built a large user base on one side of the platform, Airbnb can still grow without having to incur a great expense to encourage hosts or guests to switch platforms. However, if a local competitor builds a large user base on both sides of the platform in an important national market, Airbnb may want to consider acquiring the competitor.

If Airbnb had been founded in Germany, the regional sequence would be Europe, North America, East Asia, Africa, South Asia, and the Middle East. Note that the above sequence is predicated on the assumption that most tourism, as measured by person-trips, is domestic, followed by regional and then global. A possible alternative metric is that of overnight stays, which also results in the same ranking, though the proportions are less skewed. If one uses spending as the metric, the same priorities emerge, but with the differences becoming much smaller, as shown in figure 4.3.

While domestic tourism represents the highest percentage regardless of the metric, followed by regional tourism, these figures

Figure 4.3. European Outbound Tourism (in percentages of the total)

Destination	Trips	Nights spent	Spending
Domestic	75	58	46
Regional	19	26	33
Global	6	16	21
Total	100	100	100

Source: "Tourism Statistics, Main Destinations," Eurostat, http://ec.europa.eu/eurostat/statistics-explained/index.php/Tourism_statistics_-_top_destinations (accessed February 26, 2021).

indicate that a platform such as Airbnb should consider growing its revenue sources beyond charging a commission for each trip and/or night spent by engaging in vertical integration and product diversification, as discussed in the next section.

Airbnb's Vertical Integration and Diversification

Companies can grow organically by adding more people to their customer base, or they can try to offer existing customers more products and services—that is, by increasing their "share of wallet." This is one of the most useful concepts in marketing. A larger share of wallet not only results in higher sales but can also potentially enhance customer loyalty, and it can help the company implement highly profitable strategies such as product or service bundling. In the case of digital platforms, the benefits of share of wallet are even greater because of the central role that customer data play. If the platform can gather data on many types of customer search and purchase behaviors, as opposed to just one type, the usefulness of each bit of information grows accordingly.

Airbnb has pursued many different paths toward capturing a larger share of wallet beyond the commission it charges per rental. The company realized that both hosts and guests could be lured into buying other types of services. Hosts need services to optimize revenue from their listings, including analytics about competitors in the area, bookings, guest check-in and check-out, housekeeping and maintenance, and guest support, among others. Airbnb offers a bundle of such services for a fee. On the other side of the platform, the company offers bundling of flights, local transportation, restaurant reservations, event tickets, phone service, discount coupons, and other services.

Platforms like Airbnb can also resort to acquisitions for inorganic growth. During the 2010s, the company made vertical acquisitions in the areas of discovery platforms, social apps, reviews sites, photo blogging, scheduling apps, trip planners, social payments, and background checkers. These purchases enabled the company to include other bundled options for hosts and guests. Airbnb has also pursued acquisitions that represent a move toward related diversification, as in its purchases of companies such as Luxury Retreats and Hotel Tonight. Finally, Airbnb has engaged in horizontal acquisitions of other direct competitors in specific markets, including Accoleo in Germany and Crashpadder in the UK, both clone apps.

After years of steady growth, Airbnb has had to adjust to the pandemic. Bookings in urban areas nosedived, whereas those in more remote locations and driving-distance getaways in mountain or lakeside towns have become more popular. The extreme diversity of listings on Airbnb plays in its favor relative to hotels. The platform can offer one-family lodgings. Moreover, interactions among guests or between guests and employees are much more frequent at hotels. At the end of the day, Airbnb has real-time data on the searches and bookings people are making, which gives it an edge in terms of adapting to the new situation. Hosts can also benefit from such analytics, although the many who took out mortgages to buy city properties for rent are finding themselves in dire straits.

In fact, Airbnb is no longer a pure "sharing" platform, given that 60% of hosts have two or more listings. Preventing hosts on their side of the platform from leaving must be a top priority for Airbnb given that the density of listings is what attracts guests on the other side of the platform. One way of accomplishing that is to pivot toward longer-term stays of up to nine months, although there are dangers in such a strategy, including lower rental turnover (and thus weaker network effects) and potential backlash from regulators.

The other smart diversifying trend at Airbnb that has been intensified by the pandemic is to offer online experiences like tours, classes, and events. Many of them are offered by hosts, and they include bartending and cooking classes, makeup tutorials, comedy shows, and fortune reading. The company had launched Airbnb Experiences in 2016, offering tours, events, and activities hosted by locals. In the wake of the pandemic, this effort has gone online and grown in following. Many hosts have taken to offer online experiences directly from their homes. Some of these are free, but in most cases the cost is anywhere from a few dollars to a maximum of $65 or $75 per person and activity. Online content enables the company to turn itself into a lifestyle platform. If users interact with one another throughout the year, not only when they are planning a trip, an even greater set of network effects will be unleashed.

But the most impressive strategic initiative undertaken by Airbnb during the pandemic was to pivot away from targeting long-distance travelers to emphasizing those who wished to spend a few weeks if not months in relatively secluded areas within a few hours' drive from their home. By the summer of 2020, the platform had reached reservation levels similar to those in 2019, with average stays increasing from three or four days to seven or eight. As a result, the company reported revenue figures for the third quarter of 2020 that were nearly as high as those for the same period in 2019, after seeing a 72% decline during the second quarter. In December 2020 the company went public, its stock price surging by 112% during the first trading day, positioning it to enter one of the major stock indexes in the short term.[43]

The Platform Paradox: Things to Remember

- Unless network effects are global in nature, international expansion must proceed in a way that builds a critical mass of users in each market at the local, national, and regional levels before competitors do.
- The speed of international expansion across different local, national, and regional markets cannot exceed the speed at which the platform manages to reach critical mass and economies of scale.
- After reaching critical mass in their main line of business, platforms can diversify into new areas of revenue by increasing their share of wallet.

Chapter 5

The Limits to Platform Globalization

I n chapter 2 we explored the rise of Skype and how it had become so popular that "skype" as a verb was added to the dictionary. But during the COVID-19 pandemic, as the need to socially distance intensified, "skyping" was increasingly replaced with two other verbs: "FaceTiming" and "Zooming."

The worst mistake a digital platform can make is to take for granted that the global market is theirs if they move fast enough to leverage network effects, economies of scale, tipping points, and other similar dynamics. Ambition and hubris can become the worst enemies of international success, especially in the platform world.

Let's revisit the cases of teleconferencing and music streaming to illustrate this pitfall.

From Skype to Zoom, the Sky Is the Limit

To find platforms that actually benefit from purely global network effects, one must look in the telecommunications and teleconferencing space, where Skype, WhatsApp, and Zoom have become truly global platforms. But these are, in principle, one-sided platforms. As we saw in chapter 2, Facebook and, especially, Google's search engine are good illustrations of two-sided platforms that have managed to build a global business on the basis of global network effects.

The early success of Skype attracted many competitors. When Microsoft bought Skype in 2011, the Seattle-based giant discontinued its own platforms, Windows Live Messenger and Lyne. In 2020, Skype had 300 million monthly and 40 million daily active users, after seeing a 70% increase during the initial weeks of the coronavirus pandemic.

Still, Skype, which is mainly an application for computers, is dwarfed by the combined user base of mobile apps like WhatsApp, Facebook Messenger, WeChat, Viber, Line, KakaoTalk, and Apple's FaceTime, which in combination have over 5 billion monthly users. A major problem is that its peer-to-peer architecture does not run well on mobile devices.[44]

But Skype's global reach has been limited not only by mobile apps but also in its own turf. Zoom and Snapchat were founded in 2011, the same year Skype was acquired by Microsoft. Skype has suffered over the years not only from external competition in many markets around the world but also from Microsoft's erratic actions, from Skype for Business to incorporating Snapchat-like features and the launching of Microsoft Teams.

The growth in popularity of Zoom, mainly driven by offering an easy-to-use two-sided platform—with host(s) and participants—and free 40-minute conference calls with up to 100 attendees, offers many useful lessons. Although Skype can be used as a two-sided platform (with one participant playing the role of host or presenter), it was not designed that way. Zoom and its many competitors have benefited from the sudden relevance of remote work and learning. Still, Zoom has been plagued by considerable security problems, something that Cisco, Google, and Microsoft, to name but a few, have used to their advantage.

Two-sided digital platforms, especially those used for education and learning and thus involving teachers and students, are fundamentally different from one-sided platforms like Skype. In some cases (like Zoom), growth has been two-pronged, driven by network effects as users looked for a way to meet and share audiovisual content, and by companies and schools desperate to move their activities online. Zoom reached 300 million daily users by the end of

March 2020. But its competitors (Cisco Webex Meetings, Facebook Messenger Rooms, Google Hangouts, and Microsoft Teams) are mainly seeking to grow by offering one side of the platform (corporations and educational institutions) a product with superior performance and enhanced security.

To better understand Zoom's strategy, let's take stock of the sequence of decisions it made to expand internationally. Faced with a saturated market and formidable competitors, Zoom decided to keep it simple by offering an intuitive product with a very attractive value proposition for free users, and an easy-to-use and easy-to-deploy platform for organizations to use internally.

It invested in brand awareness through traditional means (e.g., billboards on highways) as well as digitally, and it resorted to partnerships to drive corporate adoption. By the time the pandemic struck, Zoom had offices in five US cities, as well as in Amsterdam, London, Paris, Tokyo, and Sydney. It was ready for growth in response to a global emergency. As more people downloaded the app and used it for free, the platform gained more enthusiastic users and was able to capitalize on that when negotiating with companies and schools. Zoom understood very well the two-sided nature of the platform, always looking for ways to maximize the cross-side network effects.[45]

International Expansion of (Potentially) Global Platforms

Music downloads and streaming services have proved to be immensely popular. In addition to enhancing user enthusiasm, they make tracing of sales easier, thus leading to increased copyright revenue for the artists and the music labels. After years of precipitous year-on-year declines as high as 5%, the downward trend in total revenue bottomed out in 2011. Streaming has revived the industry, increasing revenue and reducing piracy.

The Swedish company Spotify was in 2019 the largest music streaming platform, with 35% of the 360 million global subscribers, followed by Apple Music (19%), Amazon Prime Music (15%), Tencent (11%), and YouTube (6%). In addition to its nearly 120 million subscribers, Spotify boasts 140 million free, ad-supported users.[46]

Spotify is a two-sided platform, with the buyers being the listeners and the sellers being the owners of musical content. It has also launched a two-sided marketplace with listeners and creators (artists, songwriters, publishers, labels, podcasters, storytellers, etc.). It offers a catalog of 50 million songs, adding some 40,000 every day, and helps users discover music through algorithmic playlists. (Apple Music and Amazon Prime Music claim to have over 60 million songs, and Deezer some 56 million.)

In the first half of 2020, as a result of the pandemic, the numbers of both pay and free users grew by about 30%. But while the gross margin for subscribers grew from 27% to 28% year-on-year, it declined from 11% to –9% for free users, indicating a sharp decline in advertising revenue. Like Airbnb, Spotify launched its content-creation initiative a few years ago through podcasts and has accelerated it during the pandemic. The platform had 700,000 podcasts available to its listeners as of mid-2020.

While Spotify is in principle a global platform, it has grown mostly in Europe, the United States, and Latin America, with the rest of the world (regions as important as Asia, the Middle East, and Africa) representing just 16% of total users and 10% of subscribers. The company, which is headquartered in Sweden, has major operations in the United States and the UK, home to the two largest music industries in the world. Its network of sales and marketing offices includes France, Germany, the Netherlands, Norway, Spain, Canada, Australia, Brazil, Japan (another big music market), India, and Singapore.

Having a superb app and a large catalog of songs is not all a streaming platform needs, however. Attracting users is a country-by-country effort. Spotify allocates 12% of revenue to marketing and sales. Negotiating and managing partnerships is one major way in which the company attracts users, especially subscribers. It enters into agreements with equipment manufacturers and telecom companies (carriers) in which the Spotify app is preinstalled on the phones or the streaming service is bundled with others. It also has an alliance with Google Home for the US market, whereby new subscribers can get a free Google Home Mini. It bundles music with Microsoft's Xbox Game Pass in the United States and the UK. More recently, it has signed an agreement with Warner Bros. in the area of podcasts.

In music streaming, the country-by-country nature of the marketing and promotion efforts has resulted in a situation in which different platforms dominate in the various national markets. In addition, local competitors have snatched up the rights for popular local artists. In Japan, the world's second-largest recorded music market, Spotify is second to Amazon Prime Music and is followed by LINE Music, a local competitor. In South Korea, MelOn is the market leader. In China, Tencent platforms KuGou, QQ Music, and Kuwo dominate the market, which in combination have nearly 800 million users. In India, Spotify faces competition from Gaana and JioSaavn, each with over 100 million users. And in Russia, VK.com reigns supreme.

The Platform Paradox: Things to Remember

While it makes sense to think about markets from a global point of view, the reality on the ground may pose strict limitations on the extent to which companies can do business around the world as if there were no national borders. This basic principle of international management becomes even more important in the case of digital platforms because there are several boundaries, not just national ones:

- The border separating the local from the national is extremely consequential for the success of platforms built on local network effects. This is especially the case not only when users care about the situation in their specific vicinity but also when government regulation occurs mostly at the local level, as in the cases of ride hailing or casual dating.

- The frontier between the national and the regional becomes central to the effective management of digital platforms when the user in a one-sided platform, or at least one of the two types of users in a two-sided platform, is interested in crossing that boundary, as in the case of tourists or professionals looking for jobs.
- The dividing line between the regional and the global matters insomuch as users are not regionally constrained (cross-regional immigrants in the case of remittance platforms), or they wish to preserve the option of reaching other users and/or source information globally (search engines, telecommunication platforms).

Globalization is, in the end, a double-edged sword. It fragments as it integrates. It can trigger local reactions as well as worldwide dynamics. Digital platforms can't assume that there is a purely global market for their services. It may well be that the landscape looks more like a collection of separate local, national, and regional markets.

Conclusion
Three Golden Principles of International Expansion

As the platform economy continues to evolve, disruptors and incumbents alike jockey for position. Competition for information—and for the monetization of information—has become the central element in competitive strategy.

When it comes to pursuing opportunities for growth across the global economy, three golden principles stand out:

- The geographical scope of the network effects shapes the dynamic of competition in ways that show the paths to global growth.
- The platform economy requires a blend of competition and collaboration given that not even the most resourceful companies can do it all by themselves, especially when it comes to the first or last mile.
- Frequent reinvention and self-transformation are the norm for successful companies as the disruptors find themselves disrupted.

The cases of Uber and Airbnb—two of the most prominent digital platforms—indicate that international expansion is very rarely a purely global process, with Google and Zoom being among the few exceptions. The world is not flat when it comes to even some of the most globally recognizable brand names. Not only the nature of the network effects but also the level at which marketing and promotion efforts are effective—from local and national to regional and global—and exclusive sources of local content shape the sequence of expansion and the extent to which platforms become globally successful.

Digital platforms are built on the basis of network effects. Their international strategy, as we have seen, must be informed by the nature of those effects. Let's consider the four pure types of situations we encountered in chapter 2 (see figure C.1):

Figure C.1. Digital Platforms and the Sequence and Speed of Expansion into New National Markets

	Geographical scope of network effects	
	(−) Local →	Global (+)
One-sided	**Olio** • Prioritize cultural and regulatory similarities at the national and local levels. • De-emphasize small and marginal localities. • Grow at a comfortable speed and use incentives in important localities within each national market to lure users away from competitors.	**Skype** • Prioritize new, large national markets interconnected with existing markets, across all localities within each market. • Pay attention to all markets. • Grow as fast as possible in order to negate competitors' critical mass in any one market and across the world.
Two-sided	• Prioritize cultural and regulatory similarities at the national and local levels. • De-emphasize small and marginal localities. • Prevent competitors in an important locality from reaching critical mass on both sides by growing as fast as possible once a locality is entered. **Uber**	• Prioritize new, large national markets interconnected with existing markets, exploiting same-side and cross-side network effects across all localities within each market. • Pay attention to all markets. • Grow as fast as possible in order to prevent competitors from exploiting critical mass on either side. **Google**

- A one-sided food-sharing platform like Olio, driven by local network effects, can successfully establish itself in many different localities without following any specific national sequence dictated by network effects. Small or marginal localities may be left for local competitors to exploit. If a competitor builds up a presence in an important locality, lure its users away by offering incentives to switch. It would be wise, however, to follow a sequence in terms of national and local cultural or regulatory similarity to avoid unnecessary obstacles in the early stages of growth.

- A one-sided telecommunications platform like Skype, driven by global network effects, should attract users from all over the world as quickly as possible to avoid being challenged by any other platform with global ambitions or by a successful local platform situated in an important market. The best sequence to take advantage of network effects would entail prioritizing large markets with users who interact with many other users in the home country and in other markets in which the platform already has a strong position.

- A two-sided ride-hailing platform like Uber, driven by local network effects, can follow the same approach as Olio to successfully establish itself in many different localities without following any specific national sequence. But it must move faster than Olio because successful rival two-sided platforms are more difficult to dislodge from an important locality given that large numbers of drivers attract large numbers of riders, and vice versa, in a powerful self-reinforcing dynamic. Like Olio, Uber can ignore smaller or marginal localities without threatening its competitive position in larger localities or overall.

- A two-sided search and advertising platform like Google, driven by global network effects, must grow worldwide as quickly as possible to prevent other platforms from reaching a critical mass of users and companies. The best sequence to take advantage of network effects would be one that prioritizes large markets with many users and companies (on both sides of the platform) that interact with users and companies in the home country or the other markets where the platform has already established a strong presence.

Platforms operating at intermediate geographical levels (national or regional) between the extremes of local and global encountered a more complex environment regarding network effects, but also greater opportunities to grow dynamically by chasing the national and/or regional cross-side network effects.

Airbnb's case showed that a platform with international ambitions can proceed in concentric circles from the home country when it comes to generating the largest possible cross-side network effects in the shortest possible time, before any competitors gain a stronghold in some part of the world. The steps we identified in chapter 4 involve saturating the home-country market with listings to persuade more guests to join, attracting guests from other markets in the same region while at the same time reaching critical mass in listings to the benefit of home-country guests, and so on and so forth across regions in the world. At each geographical level, Airbnb maximized the cross-side network effects created by the two-sided nature of the platform.

The intermediate case of Spotify offers another key insight. The more local the marketing and promotion effort required to attract listeners and/or creators, the greater the chances that the platform will succeed only in some national markets or regions. Even further, the bigger the role of local content (as in South Korea with K-pop and other genres), the more the platform needs to heed the advice in figure C.1 concerning local network effects by prioritizing similarities at the local and national levels.

This conceptualization also applies to traditional companies that seek to transform themselves digitally: Zara, Walmart, the *New York Times*, Lego, and others. Their strategies of international digital expansion were driven by the following:

• The actions of existing competitors. For instance, in its digital transformation and expansion around the world, Zara had to benchmark against H&M and avoid falling behind it. As we saw in chapter 3, Zara implemented the rollout of its digital strategy following a sequence resulting from a mix of considerations, including distance from Spain, cultural and regulatory similarity, and size of the market. In so doing, its parent company, Inditex, is well on its way to becoming the most successful omnichannel apparel company. But its digital strategy, as in the case of Walmart, required collaboration with platforms and last-mile fulfillment services.

- The nature and actions of disruptors, and a unique value proposition. The *New York Times* played catch-up with new digital news media such as Google, Yahoo!, *Bloomberg*, Facebook, the *Huffington Post*, BuzzFeed, and many others by experimenting with different types of digital content and revenue models. Most importantly, it bet on the notion that there was demand for high-quality journalism, which is an expensive proposition. Hence the need to exploit network effects to grow nationally and internationally to make the investment pay off. That was the unique value proposition that, after many years of digital implementation through trial and error, helped the company transform itself into a viable news and analysis organization for the twenty-first century.

- The evolving relationship between the company and its customers. Lego used digital platforms to engage its customers throughout the product cycle. The strategy has generated enormous enthusiasm for the brand and created an immensely profitable intergenerational bond among Lego fans. This was how a traditional toy company became the "Apple of Toys."

Digital platforms will continue to transform the global economy. Managing them across borders requires a mindset that balances adaptation and disruption, and a thorough analysis of the underlying network effects.

Notes

All URLs were accessed on January 1, 2021.

1 Data on Amazon are from Jasmine Enberg, "Amazon Around the World," eMarketer (November 13, 2018), https://www.emarketer.com/content/amazon -around-the-world; Charles Duhigg, "Is Amazon Unstoppable?," *New Yorker* (October 21, 2019), https://www.newyorker.com/magazine/2019/10/21/is -amazon-unstoppable; Benedict Evans, "What's Amazon's Market Share?" (December 19, 2019), https://www.ben-evans.com/benedictevans/2019/12 /amazons-market-share19#:~:text=Amazon%20has%2050%25%20or%20 more,has%20never%20disclosed%20any%20data).

2 "The Speed of a Unicorn," Fleximize, https://fleximize.com/unicorns/.

3 *Global Music Report 2020* (March 6, 2020), http://www.ifpi.dk/global-music -report-2020.

4 See UNCTAD, *Digital Economy Report 2019* (New York: United Nations, 2019), https://unctad.org/en/PublicationsLibrary/der2019_en.pdf; Martin Kenney and John Zysman, "The Rise of the Platform Economy," *Issues in Science and Technology* 32, no. 3 (Spring 2016), https://issues.org/the-rise-of-the-platform -economy/; Thomas Poell, David Nieborg, and José van Dijck, "Platformisation," *Internet Policy Review* 8, no. 4 (2019), https://policyreview.info/concepts /platformisation.

5 Jonathan I. Dingel and Brent Neiman, "How Many Jobs Can Be Done at Home?," NBER Working Paper Series 26948 (2020), https://www.nber.org/papers/w26948.

6 All statistics on internet, fixed, and mobile telecommunications are from ITU, "Statistics," https://www.itu.int/en/ITU-D/Statistics/Pages/stat/default.aspx; ITU, *Measuring Digital Development: Facts and Figures 2019* (Geneva: ITU, 2019), https://www.itu.int/en/ITU-D/Statistics/Documents/facts /FactsFigures2019.pdf.

7 Some useful references on network effects include Ravi Kumar, "Understanding the Basics of Network Effects: The Power of the Platform," Medium (2018), https://medium.com/world-of-iot/understanding-the-basics-of-network-effects -the-power-of-the-platform-2cfef215fe4a; Marc Rysman, "The Economics of Two-Sided Markets," *Journal of Economic Perspectives* 23, no. 3 (Summer 2009): 125–143, https://pubs.aeaweb.org/doi/pdf/10.1257/jep.23.3.125; Jonathan A. Knee, "All Platforms Are Not Equal," *Sloan Management Review* (September 15, 2017), https://sloanreview.mit.edu/article/why-some-platforms-are-better-than-others/.

8   See https://investor.fb.com/financials/default.aspx.

9   On online dating and Tinder, see Michael Rosenfeld, Reuben J. Thomas, and Sonia Hausen, "Disintermediating Your Friends: How Online Dating in the United States Displaces Other Ways of Meeting," *Proceedings of the National Academy of Sciences* 116, no. 36 (2019), https://www.pnas.org/content/116/36/17753; Leo Sun, "How Tinder Became the Highest Grossing Mobile App of 2019," The Motley Fool (January 21, 2020), https://www.fool.com/investing/2020/01/21/how-tinder-was-highest-grossing-mobile-app-2019.aspx; Elin J. Finkel, Paul W. Eastwick, Benjamin R. Karney, Harry T. Reis, and Susan Sprecher, "Online Dating: A Critical Analysis from the Perspective of Psychological Science," *Psychology and Counseling* 13, no. 1 (2012): 3–66; Ginette Blackhart, Jennifer Fitzpatrick, and Jessica Williamson, "Dispositional Factors Predicting Use of Online Dating Sites and Behaviors Related to Online Dating," *Computers in Human Behaviour* 33 (2014): 113–118; Statista, *eServices Report 2019* (2019); Business of Apps, "Tinder Revenue and User Statistics 2020," http://www.businessofapps.com/data/tinder-statistics/#2.

10 Rosenfeld, Thomas, and Hausen, "Disintermediating Your Friends."

11 See https://www.collinsdictionary.com/us/dictionary/english/uberize. On Uber's approach to regulation, see Marcus Wohlsen, "Uber's Brilliant Strategy to Make Itself Too Big to Ban," *Wired* (July 8, 2014); Andy Kessler, "Travis Kalanick: The Transportation Trustbuster," *Wall Street Journal* (January 25, 2013); Sam Knight, "How Uber Conquered London," *Guardian* (April 27, 2016).

12 See https://www.collinsdictionary.com/us/submission/17695/Uberization.

13 Kessler, "Travis Kalanick."

14 Raghav Singh, "The Rise and Fall of Monster," ERE (August 9, 2016), https://www.ere.net/the-rise-and-fall-of-monster/.

15 See https://www.statista.com/statistics/967713/online-jobs-market-firms-worldwide/.

16 Knomad, *Leveraging Economic Migration for Development* (August 2019), https://www.knomad.org/publication/leveraging-economic-migration-development-briefing-world-bank-board.

17 See World Bank, "Migration and Remittances," https://www.worldbank.org/en/topic/labormarkets/brief/migration-and-remittances.

18 "The Secret of Zara's Success," MartinRoll Business & Brand Leadership (2020), https://martinroll.com/resources/articles/strategy/the-secret-of-zaras-success-a-culture-of-customer-co-creation/; Felipe Caro and Jeremie Gallien, "Inventory Management of a Fast-Fashion Retail Network," *Operations Research* 58 (2010): 257–273.

19 Euromonitor International Lifestyle Survey 2019, *World Market for Apparel and Footwear* (2019). On the digital transformation of apparel manufacturing and retail, see Statista, *Apparel Report 2019*.

20 On Zara's digital transformation, see Susana Rois, "Historia de Inditex Online," Marketing 4 Ecommerce (December 2020), https://marketing4ecommerce.net /historia-inditex-online-ecommerce-moda/; Felipe Caro and Jeremie Gallien, "Inventory Management of a Fast-Fashion Retail Network," *Operations Research* 58 (2010): 257–273; José Antonio Miranda, "The Country-of-Origin Effect and the International Expansion of Spanish Fashion Companies, 1975–2015," *Business History* (October 2017): 488–508; BDB Team, "How Does Zara Survive Despite Minimal Advertising?" (January 23, 2019), https://www.billiondollarboy .com/news/zara-influencer-marketing/.

21 "Judith McKenna Discusses Walmart's International Business, Global Perception, Weighs In on Trade Disputes," Yahoo! Finance (June 5, 2019), https://finance.yahoo.com/video/judith-mckenna-discusses-walmarts -international-155521326.html.

22 Statista, *Global eServices Report 2020*.

23 On the digital disruption of the printed media, see Pew Research Center, "Newspapers Fact Sheet" (July 9, 2019), https://www.journalism.org/fact-sheet /newspapers/; Felix Simon and Lucas Graves, "Across Seven Countries, the Average Price for Paywalled News Is About $15.75/month," NiemanLab (May 8, 2019), https://www.niemanlab.org/2019/05/across-seven-countries-the-average -price-for-paywalled-news-is-about-15-75-month/.

24 See Keach Hagey, Lukas I. Alpert, and Yaryna Serkez, "In News Industry, a Stark Divide Between Haves and Have-Nots," *Wall Street Journal* (May 4, 2019), https://www.wsj.com/graphics/local-newspapers-stark-divide/.

25 See Hagey, Alpert, and Serkez, "In News Industry"; Gabriel Snyder, "*The New York Times* Claws Its Way into the Future," *Wired* (December 2, 2017).

26 Hagey, Alpert, and Serkez, "In News Industry."

27 The data on book sales by format are from BookScan and Statista, *Book Formats in the U.S.* (2019), https://www.statista.com/topics/3938/book-formats-in-the-us/.

28 Andrew Perrin, "Book Reading 2016," Pew Research Center (September 1, 2016), https://www.pewresearch.org/internet/2016/09/01/book-reading-2016/.

29 Ferris Jabr, "The Reading Brain in the Digital Age: The Science of Paper versus Screens," *Scientific American* (April 11, 2013).

30 Edward Tenner, "Why People Stick with Outdated Technology," *Scientific American* (November 24, 2015).

31 The data on wine sales by channel are from the Passport GMID database.

32 Julie Bower, "The Evolution of the UK Wine Market: From Niche to Mass-Market Appeal," *Beverages* (November 2018), https://www.mdpi.com/2306-5710 /4/4/87/pdf.

33 Mary Blackiston, "How Lego Went from Nearly Bankrupt to the Most Powerful Brand in the World," Success Agency, https://www.successagency.com/growth

/2018/02/27/lego-bankrupt-powerful-brand/; Lucy Handley, "How Marketing Built Lego into the World's Favorite Toy Brand," CNBC (April 27, 2018), https://www.cnbc.com/2018/04/27/lego-marketing-strategy-made-it-world -favorite-toy-brand.html; Johnny Davis, "How Lego Clicked: The Super Brand That Reinvented Itself," *Guardian* (June 4, 2017); Jonathan Ringen, "How Lego Became the Apple of Toys," *Fast Company* (August 1, 2015); David Kindy, "How Lego Patents Helped Build a Toy Empire, Brick by Brick," *Smithsonian Magazine* (February 7, 2019).

34 Jeff Beer, "The Secret to Lego's Social Media Success Is in the Creative Power of Crowds," *Fast Company* (June 20, 2017).

35 David Kindy, "How Lego Patents Helped Build a Toy Empire, Brick by Brick," *Smithsonian Magazine* (February 7, 2019).

36 David C. Robertson, *Brick by Brick: How LEGO Rewrote the Rules of Innovation and Conquered the Global Toy Industry* (New York: Crown Business, 2013).

37 M. Irtash Sohail, *Lego Brand Audit Report* (2020), https://pdfcoffee.com/lego -audit-reportdocx-pdf-free.html.

38 Oberlo, "Search Engine Market Share in 2020," https://www.oberlo.com /statistics/search-engine-market-share#:~:text=Handling%20over%2090%20 percent%20of,done%20through%20the%20internet%20giant.

39 Quoted in Kari Paul, "Millennials Are Trying to Redefine What It Means to Be an American Tourist Abroad," MarketWatch (October 5, 2017), https://www .marketwatch.com/story/what-we-can-all-learn-from-millennials-about-travel -2017-10-04.

40 All statistics on Airbnb's users are from Statista's database.

41 World Bank, World Development Indicators Database (2021), https://datatopics .worldbank.org/world-development-indicators/; OECD, Tourism Statistics (2021), https://www.oecd.org/cfe/tourism/tourism-statistics.htm.

42 Statistics on tourism are from OECD Statistics Database, https://stats.oecd.org /Index.aspx?DataSetCode=TOURISM_DOMESTIC; U.S. Travel Association, "U.S. Travel and Tourism Overview 2019," https://www.ustravel.org/system/files /media_root/document/Research_Fact-Sheet_US-Travel-and-Tourism -Overview.pdf; Eurostat, "Tourism Statistics—Top Destinations," http://ec .europa.eu/eurostat/statistics-explained/index.php/Tourism_statistics_-_top _destinations; United Nations World Tourism Organization, "Statistics," https://www.unwto.org/statistics; International Trade Administration, "Fast Facts: United States Travel and Tourism Industry 2019," https://travel.trade.gov /outreachpages/download_data_table/Fast_Facts_2019.pdf.

43 Airbnb's response to the pandemic is analyzed in Tarik Dogru, Makarand Mody, Courtney Suess, and Nathan Line, "Airbnb 2.0: Is It a Sharing Economy Platform or a Lodging Corporation?," *Tourism Management* 78 (June 2020), https://www.researchgate.net/publication/337573893_Airbnb_20_Is_it_a _sharing_economy_platform_or_a_lodging_corporation; Jill Menze, "People

Are Staying Longer in Airbnbs—for Now," *PhocusWire* (May 20, 2020), https://www.phocuswire.com/airbnb-long-term-stays-on-rise; James Ware, "I Tried 80 Airbnb Online 'Experiences,' and It Was Actually an Adventure," *Slate* (June 20, 2020), https://slate.com/technology/2020/06/80-airbnb-online-experience-one-week.html.

44 Tom Warren, "Microsoft's Skype Struggles Have Created a Zoom Moment," The Verge (March 31, 2020), https://www.theverge.com/2020/3/31/21200844/microsoft-skype-zoom-houseparty-coronavirus-pandemic-usage-growth-competition.

45 Ashley Carman, "Why Zoom Became So Popular," The Verge (April 3, 2020), https://www.theverge.com/2020/4/3/21207053/zoom-video-conferencing-security-privacy-risk-popularity.

46 See Spotify, Form 6-K (July 2020), http://d18rn0p25nwr6d.cloudfront.net/CIK-0001639920/818bc571-7eb0-4959-bc59-bff08fe6a2a0.pdf.

Index

About the Author

Mauro F. Guillén is Dean of the Cambridge Judge Business School and Professor Emeritus at the Wharton School of the University of Pennsylvania, where he was the holder of the Zandman Endowed Professorship in International Management. He served as Director of the Lauder Institute of Management & International Studies between 2007 and 2019.

He received a PhD in sociology from Yale University and a doctorate in political economy from the University of Oviedo in his native Spain.

He is a trustee of the Royal Foundation of Spain, known as the Fundación Princesa de Asturias, and a member of the advisory board of the Escuela de Finanzas Aplicadas (Grupo Analistas). He serves on advisory groups at the World Economic Forum.

He has won the Aspen Institute's Faculty Pioneer Award. He is an elected fellow of the Sociological Research Association and of the Macro Organizational Behavior Society, a former Guggenheim and Fulbright Fellow, and a member in the Institute for Advanced Study at Princeton. In 2005 he won the IV Fundación Banco Herrero Prize, awarded annually to the best Spanish social scientist under the age of 40. He has delivered the Clarendon Lectures at Oxford University, the Otto Krause Memorial Lecture at the University of Johannesburg, and the Laurent Picard Distinguished Lecture at McGill University.

He has received a Wharton MBA Core Teaching Award, a Wharton Graduate Association Teaching Award, a Wharton Teaching Commitment and Curricular Innovation Award, the Gulf Publishing Company Best Paper Award of the Academy of

Management, the W. Richard Scott Best Paper Award of the American Sociological Association, the Gustavus Myers Center Award for Outstanding Book on Human Rights, and the President's Book Award of the Social Science History Association.

His current research deals with digital platforms, the internationalization of the firm, and the impact of globalization on patterns of organization and on the diffusion of innovations and crises. His most recent books are *The Platform Paradox: How Digital Businesses Succeed in an Ever-Changing Global Marketplace* (2021), *2030: How Today's Biggest Trends Will Collide and Reshape the Future of Everything* (2020), *The Architecture of Collapse: The Global System in the Twenty-First Century* (2016), *Global Turning Points* (2012), and *Emerging Markets Rule* (2012).

About Wharton School Press

Wharton School Press, the book publishing arm of the Wharton School of the University of Pennsylvania, was established to inspire bold, insightful thinking within the global business community.

Wharton School Press publishes a select list of award-winning, best-selling, and thought-leading books that offer trusted business knowledge to help leaders at all levels meet the challenges of today and the opportunities of tomorrow. Led by a spirit of innovation and experimentation, Wharton School Press leverages groundbreaking digital technologies and has pioneered a fast-reading business book format that fits readers' busy lives, allowing them to swiftly emerge with the tools and information needed to make an impact. Wharton School Press books offer guidance and inspiration on a variety of topics, including leadership, management, strategy, innovation, entrepreneurship, finance, marketing, social impact, public policy, and more.

Wharton School Press also operates an online bookstore featuring a curated selection of influential books by Wharton School faculty and Press authors published by a wide range of leading publishers.

To find books that will inspire and empower you to increase your impact and expand your personal and professional horizons, visit *wsp.wharton.upenn.edu.*

About the Wharton School

Founded in 1881 as the world's first collegiate business school, the Wharton School of the University of Pennsylvania is shaping the future of business by incubating ideas, driving insights, and creating leaders who change the world. With a faculty of more than 235 renowned professors, Wharton has 5,000 undergraduate, MBA, Executive MBA, and doctoral students. Each year 13,000 professionals from around the world advance their careers through Wharton Executive Education's individual, company-customized, and online programs. More than 99,000 Wharton alumni form a powerful global network of leaders who transform business every day.

For more information, visit *www.wharton.upenn.edu.*

CPSIA information can be obtained
at www.ICGtesting.com
Printed in the USA
BVHW081110010821
613366BV00007B/591